T0105650

TRANSFORMING FEAR AND ANXIETY INTO *POWER*

Life Lessons and the Path to Healing

Workbook Included

Janice M. Mann

BALBOA
PRESS

A DIVISION OF HAY HOUSE

Balboa Press books may be ordered through booksellers or by contacting:

Balboa Press
A Division of Hay House
1663 Liberty Drive
Bloomington, IN 47403
www.balboapress.com
1-(877) 407-4847

Because of the dynamic nature of the Internet, any web addresses or links contained in this book may have changed since publication and may no longer be valid. The views expressed in this work are solely those of the author and do not necessarily reflect the views of the publisher, and the publisher hereby disclaims any responsibility for them.

The author of this book does not dispense medical advice or prescribe the use of any technique as a form of treatment for physical, emotional, or medical problems without the advice of a physician, either directly or indirectly. The intent of the author is only to offer information of a general nature to help you in your quest for emotional and spiritual well-being. In the event you use any of the information in this book for yourself, which is your constitutional right, the author and the publisher assume no responsibility for your actions.

Any people depicted in stock imagery provided by Thinkstock are models, and such images are being used for illustrative purposes only.
Certain stock imagery © Thinkstock.

ISBN: 978-1-4525-5950-6 (sc)
ISBN: 978-1-4525-5951-3 (e)

Printed in the United States of America

Balboa Press rev. date: 09/19/2012

CONTENTS

DEDICATION

This book is dedicated to all those spiritual beings having a human experience that I have met, created relationships with, journeyed along beside, loved, lost, forgiven, loved more and learned incredibly powerful life lessons along side. You know who you are.

ACKNOWLEDGMENTS

There are a few very sacred relationships that have helped me to get to this point. First and foremost, this book is a testimony to the love of my incredibly patient, generous and unconditionally loving mother, Macel "Mitzie" Mann. Without her devotion and guidance I would either be dead, in jail or in a psychiatric hospital. There are no words to convey my profound gratitude that she is my mother. May she rest in the total peace of the Everlasting Arms of God. I will see you on the Other Side, Mama.

Thank you with all of my heart to Lisa L. Cogar for being the best friend I have ever had. You have loved unconditionally and taught me so much more about compassion than I have ever known. You held me through night terrors, recurring violent nightmares, post traumatic based stress, coaxed me down during panic attacks and anxiety attacks and never made me feel less than. You have housed me in fragile moments and always treated me fairly even when I did not treat you in the same way. You are my teacher. I love you!

Special thanks to Dorothy Hand who has spent twelve years being my great friend, storm watcher and prayer partner.

Last but not least, a very special thanks to Geraldine Scott who has been by my side as a tremendous friend through some awesome growing experiences!

You are sacred gifts in my life! I am grateful for your love!

This book would not be here without the messages received by my sister, Mary Mann Carington Smith. Mary listened when no one else would. She allowed me to be in my stuff and work through it. She offered me shelter in a hell of a storm. May she Rest in Peace! Keep sending the messages! Special Thanks to Author K'Anne Meinel and to Jennifer Valeri for all their assistance to this project.

NOTES

The Workbook is in the back of the book. Words in italics are differentiated from the text as they are self study questions to provide the reader with guided thoughts for additional experiential insight.

Warning: Reading this book may cause the quality of your life to be changed for the better forever!

Janice Mann is available for public speaking engagements, trainings, seminars or private consultations. Contact her at JMannconsulting@verizon.net.

INTRODUCTION

The fact that you are reading these words tells me that you are open to learning more, growing, changing and healing. You are in the right place, at the right time, and reading the right information. It is my belief that you wouldn't be here now if you were not ready to take this information in, absorb what you need and then share it with others. This is part of a Divine Plan. Your reading this book will give you unique and beneficial answers to questions I had to answer for myself without you struggling.

Synchronicity is defined by Carl Jung as "the coming together of inner and outer events in a way that cannot be explained by cause and effect and that is meaningful to the observer." Synchronicity is why you are reading this now. It is time for you to have this information to make you stronger and make your journey easier and better.

It is my belief that you need to hear the message from your Inner Intelligence. Your fears are screaming at you so loud and so profound that you are struggling to cope with anxiety attacks, irrational fears, phobias, depression and more. It is time to have a spiritual transformation so that you can be all You were created to be. The spiritual, psychological and behavioral based strategies in this book are here to help you shift your dependence on exterior and outer things and learn to trust yourself, your intuition and your Inner Intelligence. Going Within and tapping your power is one of the most profoundly positive changes you can learn to create in your life! Raising your Spiritual Consciousness will decrease and may terminate your irrational fear based thoughts over time. The end result will be you owning your own power, living peacefully with your own comfortable thoughts and creating your own world. This will be a huge transformation internally.

I am not talking about religion. I am talking about Spirituality. It has been said that "Religion is for people afraid of going to hell. Spirituality is for people who have already been there." Becoming mindful and aware of how you feel and how you choose to respond to situations will raise your consciousness.

I no longer believe in coincidences. Everything in the Universe happens for a reason. We don't always know why or understand why something is happening. It happens. We are exactly where we need to be. We get the opportunity to learn about ourselves and others while we attempt to figure out why and how. The solution is to ask the Inner Intelligence, the Holy Spirit Within, your Higher Power, for help and a new direction. An answer will come if we quiet our minds and listen. We must suspend our fears, judgments and negative thinking and trust that we are moving forward in the right direction.

I have spent the major part of my life dealing with irrational fears and anxiety to the point of polarizing Panic Disorder, Depression and Post Traumatic Stress Disorder. Childhood abuse, self sabotaging medicated drug abuse, self-loathing, a heightened sense of abandonment and betrayal, incredibly deep and profound emotional pain along with both of my parents having suffered from depression brought me to a very deep ravine of doubt, fear, anxiety, panic and grief. The outer world is a product of our inner dialogue. I have found my way out of the wilderness and hope to help you help yourself to do the same.

So just trust the process. Read the book. Do the exercises if you want to get additional insight via more experiential knowledge. It's all your choice. Make an intentional choice to heal yourself for you are the only one who can.

Are you courageous enough to transform belief into realization? You already are transforming belief when you focus on worry, stress, anxiety and fear. You just need to learn how to turn this process around and empower yourself through the process by taking the very same energy that you have used to tell yourself all the negative fear based thoughts and start changing them to positive love based thoughts. You have to learn how to talk yourself down from the anxiety and panic into a place of serenity.

I encourage you to notice when you start feeling resistant to what you are reading. Make a note of it in a notebook. Resistance can mean that you are coming up against a thought that has FEAR underneath of it. Ask yourself: "What am I feeling? Why am I feeling this way? How is it manifesting in my mind and body? Are you noticing physical symptoms? Does your stomach hurt? Are you instantly bored? Are you getting a headache? Do you feel sad? Mad? Scared? Worried? Anxious? "Notice your process. It is your personal process. You can't do it wrong or right. You don't need to be concerned about getting it right. Just do it. Take notes. Pause when you need to. Relax into your process. It does not have to be stressful. This is your journey.

1

MY STORY

I was the baby in the family. I was Daddy's little girl. The Sun rose and fell on him in my eyes. I was a sickly child. I was hospitalized yearly numerous times for pneumonia and bronchitis. I was sick and home from school often. He worked a schedule where he was the significant caretaker for me because my Mom was teaching at the local Elementary School. He could free his schedule up to take care of doctor visits and home care. I adored my father. He would work deals with me that if I would be brave and take the shots at the doctor's office, then he would buy the ginger ale and a Casper or Richie Rich Comic Book at the local corner drug store when he filled my prescriptions. We understood each other as well as any energy sensitive child can understand their primary caregiver. I modeled most of his behaviors. My father was incredibly charismatic, intelligent and empathic. He had a great sense of humor, had a calming effect on others, had southern hospitality, had never met a stranger and was a strong presence in every room. He went out of his way to make me laugh. We were incredibly close for my formative years.

My father was a well known minister in the community. We lived in a very small town in the mountains where everyone thought they knew your business. Gossip and rumors ran amuck. I was a precocious child with a great intellect. However, I didn't understand why my father was drinking alcohol, acting different, eating handfuls of pills, and later being psychiatrically hospitalized against his will. Things changed quickly when they changed. I couldn't fathom a life different than the one I had lived to this point. For a few years, it was very scary for me because he would come home apologetic, be charming, get mad and move out, come back drunk yelling and beating on the doors in the middle of the night, begging for forgiveness, then fighting with my mom, leave, come home again crying, leave again. Totally erratic! He smelled bad (alcohol). I didn't know what it was at first. The strongest drink allowed in our home had been root beer.

I didn't understand how or why my father the Minister, could have gotten his young, college age, part-time church secretary pregnant. She had lived with us for a summer and had a crush on my father. It only took one manic episode for all hell to break loose.

He would get verbally, emotionally and physically abusive with my mom, my brother and I. I didn't know this monster man who had taken over the body and mind of my daddy. I just cried and shook. He would try to come and calm me down whenever he felt guilty because he would see me shaking. It made him mad if I didn't become immediately soothed in appearance. There was no safety in his presence. Life had changed forever.

My father would show up drunk at the Christmas Eve church service my mother took us too after the separation. He would sit behind us in the pews. I could smell the alcohol on his breath. It was fear producing because no one knew what he would do next. I think his guilt ate him up over time.

He would show up as a substitute teacher in my school. I would go to the principal's office for the day because I couldn't go home sick. I felt entrapped in a school with a man who had tried to kill me. Walking down the hall and seeing him at a classroom doorway just put me into panic and confusion. I couldn't take the stress.

I never thought my parents would divorce. My mother took her wedding vows seriously. Nor did I think that to get my mother to give my father a divorce he would attempt premeditated murder! I took the phone call from him that morning and without realizing it had told him we were going to be home that evening alone. I had let him know we would be vulnerable. Talk about child-like guilt gone wild.

He snuck into the side yard after dark and cut the phone lines. Later, he forced his way into our house and pulled a large, well sharpened, hunting knife on my mother and brother. He forced them go to the bedroom where I was sleeping peacefully. He pushed the furniture against the bedroom doors so no one could get in or go out. I woke up to him pacing, frothing at the mouth, crying, begging, angry, yelling, all at once; while simultaneously yielding a knife, meant for death, back and forth between the three of us.

My mother kept moving back and forth between my brother and me to protect us from his insanity. Time stood still. I remember looking at our Maryland house windows that were so high up. There was no way out.

I will be eternally grateful to my maternal grandmother, Mary Cogar Baughman, and the Maryland State Troopers who saved my family's lives. Domestic violence protective orders are just paper. They mean nothing to a crazy man. I waited by the windows in our home for weeks and months on end, biting my nails, waiting, watching, anticipating him coming back to finish us off. Nightmares and night terrors kept me from good sleep for years. Fear had an entirely new meaning. At ten, I understood the term "terror" for the first time in my life.

There are still times when I am overtired that I can still see his shadow standing in the doorway, forty years and tens of thousands of dollars in therapy later. I know fear, anxiety and terror. My childlike Magical Mind thought somehow we got a pass for the bad stuff in life because he and my mother had been devoting their life to "God's work"! (and much of mine…can you imagine how much Sunday School and Bible School I had to attend being the child of a five country church circuit minister?) I didn't understand how God could let my hard working, dedicated, loyal, loving Mother become so heartbroken, grief so deep she became depressed and wanted to die. On top of that, my best friend forever, Missy, died in a car accident with her dad, another minister, on the way back from running shopping errands. I questioned whether there was some kind of hit list for ministers and their kids. It was my childlike Magical Thinking gone wild. Can you imagine what my story looked like to me? I just didn't understand. If God loved me so much how could all this happen to me by age ten?

I was angry at the God of my understanding. I began using and abusing drugs and alcohol to self medicate my pain in my early teens. What was real and what was not real? Was God's love real? Where was it?

I had a death wish for years. In my thinking if my own father didn't love me then I was not worthy of love. He had meant everything to me. He was long gone with a new family. That was adding insult to injury. I projected my anger at my mother because my father was gone. Unfortunately for her, she was safe enough for me to rage against regularly. I was as hateful and raging as any rage-a-holic could be toward her. I was rude, angry and able to articulate my deepest negative thoughts and project them all on my mother. My emotional pain was so deep and so real that, starting at fourteen, I just wanted to stay as high as I could for as long as I could.

It took many years of substance abuse, danger buzzes, hangovers, blackouts, and overdoses to begin to deal with the real root issues. I had stuffed down incredible rage. I had isolated myself from my mother and brother. Thank God I had an older sister who cared. My brother was protective of me when I was young. However, once I hit the teenage rage stage his response was to attempt to be intimidating and say unkind things to me. He has his own pain. I didn't understand how he could respond in that manner. I had some serious pain and woundedness to work out. Just like you. I have worked on me for quite some time. You can heal yourself, too! I have learned that out of my deepest despair have come my greatest gifts.

Chapter One Workbook Exercises

Have you been abused or mistreated? How do you handle the memories that are hurtful? Do you talk to anyone about it? Do you write your thoughts and feelings in a journal? Have you realized that you are not at fault? Do you have some kind of support system to help facilitate healing for you for these situations?

2

THE WOUNDED SELF

It is hard to admit we are wounded. It is hard to admit we have lost our way. The truth is some of us have never truly found our way yet. Some people are still searching. The good news is that if you are still searching you have not given up hope in finding your way. There is always hope even when it is your experience not to have been seeking it. That is called grace.

I can speak from my personal experience and from those of others I have worked with over thirty five years of working with people. In my experience, the wounded self has some of these symptoms: lack of confidence, uncomfortable in new environments, unchecked rage, feeling as if they are not enough, fatigue, digestion issues, high irritability, moodiness, queasy stomach conditions, profound sadness without understanding why, feelings of nervousness, irrational fear, a tendency to have headaches and stiff joint pain, anxiety, lack of flexibility in decision making, lack of accountability in your actions and choices, willingness to blame others, a sense of unreasonable entitlement, low self-esteem, low sense of self love, relationships that are conditional versus unconditionally loving, you make sure you bail from the love relationship you are in before they can leave you, fears of abandonment are deeply rooted in your psyche, you have a strong sense of betrayal by others, co-dependency issues, a false facade or false self put on for the public to see, a desire to be in control whenever possible, feelings of shame, guilt, resentment and embarrassment. You do not have to have all of these symptoms to qualify. While you are reading this you will know how you are feeling. You will know if you self qualify by your own truth.

I would bet that you are either this person or love a person that is dealing with these issues or you would not be reading this book. Let me explain some of this for you.

You are in pain when you are emotionally wounded. You ache - emotionally, as in heartache and physically, as in body aches. You are afraid. You lie. You lie about lying. You cannot have self confidence because you do not believe in yourself. You feel as if you are a failure. You do not feel strong and empowered. You feel fragile and afraid. You question yourself on decisions. You overcompensate for this by acting as if you are in control. In truth, you are absolutely not in control of yourself and your feelings. There is not a true point of personal power within you. You have no idea what personal empowerment is when you are struggling. It is completely out of your experience.

You find that you are tired regularly. It takes a tremendous amount of your energy to get through each day because you have not figured out yet how to transform your fears and anxiety into power. It is likely that you don't eat as nutritiously as you could. It is likely that you have a high intake of sugars and junk food. You do not feed your body well enough to fuel yourself in a healthy manner. Perhaps you take prescription drugs for emotional issues. Perhaps you drink too much alcohol. Perhaps you smoke pot to chill out. It is likely that some of you smoke cigarettes in an attempt to center yourself. Bottom line is that you do not take care of yourself. Why? Self love and self care are low on your priorities!

Most of you transfer your sense of safety to external controls. You make up a story about what personal success looks like for you. You buy lots of things to make you feel better about yourself. Sometimes you choose the role of a victim or the role of a martyr. You find that this is easier that choosing to heal yourself. It looks like you are lazy to some. In truth, you are so paralyzed with fear that you throw an attitude rather than deal with yourself. Sarcasm prevails rather than compliments and kindness.

You need to learn the internal controls, but, that would first take motivation and desire. You are not likely to make changes until you are pushed to your limit and are frightened beyond your comfort zone. Change happens when we are ready to surrender to the process. Change happens when the pain to stay in the same situation is bigger than the perceived pain you think it is going to be for change. Change happens when your desperation become greater than your comfort zone or your discomfort zone.

It is likely that for years you have stuffed down your true feelings. Heartache at four years old feels as bad as heartache at forty years old. At forty years old, however, you have had years of stuffing the pain down inside you. Holding on to your woundedness, anger and rage festers inside of you causing disease and dis-ease. Not being at ease in yourself is dis-ease. Woundedness is converted from emotional pain to rage and anger. You find it is much easier to deal with anger. In anger, you don't feel as vulnerable. People can become afraid of you rather than the other way around. You may intimidate and manipulate your family and friends with your rage. There is an illusion of power in scaring people into doing things for you. You fall into the illusion that some sense of power is better than no sense of power. You can be vicious; either to yourself or others or both. Your behavior depends upon your emotional pain in the moment.

Then again, you may be isolating and not want to talk or be around others. You may believe that the less you have to deal with other people's energies and issues the better. You shut yourself off from family and friends. You choose to not go out to events. You avoid leaving your home. You may even feel, at times, that people unrealistically are out to hurt you or get you. This is called paranoia. You hide in your own small world and avoid contact with others. You wish things were different. You don't have a clue how to make things change. You believe you don't have what it takes within you to make those changes even if you did know how to make them. You self sabotage yourself on a regular basis. Your mind is a desperate place to be.

Does any of this resonate with you? It is a painful existence. The good news is that change can be made. You don't have to be unhappy. You can create a new story for yourself. You can face your fears and free yourself from this negative fear based thinking that has paralyzed you. You can get free of your addictions. You can learn new behaviors and coping skills. You can see your world from a transformed space of love rather than fear. The questions now become: "Are you willing to do the work? Are you willing to change old patterns of thinking? Are you willing to be risk taking for your success and health? Can you trust that there is something bigger that you have not yet found that could help you? Do you have the courage to change?

Chapter Two Workshop Exercise

In the book there are lots of examples of behaviors for people who are emotionally wounded. Review that section and then write down three symptoms or descriptions that you feel define you now.

3
LOVE VERSUS FEAR

Transforming irrational fear, anxiety and worry into your own empowerment can be accomplished. Folks are doing it every day. I have walked this journey into transformation of my fears and anxieties to personal empowerment. I am constantly working on it to get clearer, feel stronger and have a better sense of well-being. It takes some willingness to learn and desire to change. You are already half way there if you have both of those desires inside of you! Feeling and standing in your own power will be an awesome experience. Now is the time to let go of irrational fear, worry and anxiety. Once you start making the shifts in consciousness the anxiety and fear based thoughts begin to go away. At some point in your future, if you do your own emotional work, you will just remember that in the past, you used to have anxiety and panic attacks. You will not be actively fearful like you were in the past or may be now. It becomes part of your history, but, not of your current story.

Choosing love over fear is a process. A choice if you will. I realized years ago that if I was not going to control my thoughts that somebody else would. Think about it. When we are children, we are taught what our culture has taught to generations upon generations of people. We are taught religious values, social values, moral values, educational values and community values. There is usually a sense of duality as part of the process. When I say this what I mean is that there is "good" behavior or culturally approved behavior. There is "bad" behavior or culturally disapproved behavior.

I found I didn't agree with what I was being taught. It did not resonate with me. So I decided I wanted to be in control of my thoughts. That meant I had to be held accountable to myself for my thoughts. It meant that it didn't matter anymore what the church said, the school said, my parents said or the community said. I had to be the bottom line of choosing my thoughts and feeling comfortable with my choices. It meant that I had to rethink all my major belief systems and decide which ones worked for me and which ones to discard because they did not work for me any longer. It took me time to learn these new improved thinking patterns. That singular act took incredible courage and had significant spiritual ramifications. In some form I was having a revolution internally. Self knowledge results in choice and actions never taken previously. I had made a significant decision even though I wasn't aware enough to know what was in store for me on my journey.

For the purposes of this book, let's agree that there are basically two thought patterns to deal with in the Universe. Love and Fear. They both hold strong energy. However, Love energy is ultimately the strongest energy and can transform fear. The oppostite of love is not hate. It is indifference. Hate cannot exist where love is recognized. You may have been taught differently. You may have been taught different describing words. Go with the flow here and see if this helps rather than getting all worked up because what I am saying is not what you are comfortable hearing. All choices come from these two thought patterns.

In the, 13th Chapter of Corinthians in the New Testament, also known as the Love Chapter, Paul defines Love. "Love is patient and kind; it is not jealous; it does not boast; it is not arrogant; it does not act with rudeness and does not seek its own way. Love is not provoked; it never harbors ill will and is never glad when wrong is done. It bears up under anything. It exercises faith in everything. It keeps up hope in everything. It gives us power to endure anything. Love never fails."

For example, Love could include joy, loving, wisdom, serenity, abundance, harmony, well being, compassion, kindness, peace, trust, The Soul, Source Energy, God, Teachings of the Buddha, Teachings of Jesus, Holy Spirit, Teachings of Allah, Mother Earth Energy, The Universe, Christ Consciousness, Inner Intelligence etc. Pick any name because they are all in the same category. They all come from the same Source. We want to feel good. To truly feel good we need to feel loved. We need to feel connected to the Divine within us. God is manifest in all we are and all we do that comes from Love.

When I was in my twenties, I heard this quote by Les Brown: "Feed your faith and your doubt will starve to death." I have found that you cannot be present in fear and in love at the same time. You cannot be trusting and afraid simultaneously. You are either in one state of thinking or in the other. The best news is that YOU get to make the choice where you put your energy!

Fear and anxiety can be mastered. Everyone experiences fear and anxiety. When you are in fear and anxiety you are in pain. When you are in pain you can be frightened. Frightened people can be terribly vicious to others, but, especially vicious to themselves. Rarely are we upset for the reason we think we are upset. What you believe for yourself is true for you. You can make up any story or series of illusions that you want. Why make up stories that cause you pain? I believe that some of us do it because we are wounded. We keep the self loathing story going because we haven't forgiven ourselves for not being perfect. We must acknowledge the Light within us for us to change. Darkness cannot survive when light is present. To transform fear and anxiety into your own empowerment you have to raise your personal awareness and raise your spiritual consciousness. My definition of raising your consciousness is knowing and intentionally choosing to learn to release the old messages and stories that you have held in your being; embrace new thoughts that feel better and create your new story now; know ultimately that whatever ends for you is ending at the highest and best moment for you; and being aware that something new will always arrive after letting go of the old stories.

Fear has two types: Rational fear and irrational fear. Examples of responses that are fear based are jealousy, anxiety, hatred, anger, frustration, animosity, retaliation, a sense of lacking in self, guilt, shame, scarcity, brokenness, pride, greed, seeing yourself as damaged goods, criticism, insecurity, low self esteem, self-hatred, anxiety, poverty mentality, doubt etc. The answers to fear based responses are compassion and love.

A Course in Miracles, Chapter 2, Verse 27 says "When you are afraid of anything you are acknowledging its power to hurt you." The Truth is whatever you are afraid of is based in fear. What you resist persists. What you face fades. FEAR has been an acronym for False Evidence Appearing Real. Think on that. The Truth is that you are responsible for what you think because you have choices. Why do you condone irrational thinking?

Looking for help to stopping fear is not the route to get to where you want to be. Looking at the conditions of how the fear came about is how you heal yourself. Look deep within. "The Course, Chapter Two, Verse 27, goes on to say that "Fear is always a sign of strain, arising whenever what you want conflicts with what you do." Only your mind can produce fear. The empowerment process guarantees that you can control your mind by tapping into your Divinity. Thought and belief can be combined into such a power surge that it can literally move mountains. You can release fear as soon as you understand where it comes from and what is lacking. Give yourself what is lacking and you become empowered. Give yourself Love.

Rational fear (Healthy fear) is defined by Wikipedia as a strong unpleasant emotion that causes a person to retreat when confronted by danger, difficulty, opposition or pain. Example: You see a car coming at you at a high speed while you are walking in the road. Your heart starts to race and you feel afraid. You have sensed danger. You move out of the way so you will not get hit by the car. The danger feeling ends. The adrenaline rush disappears. This is healthy fear.

Irrational fear (Unhealthy fear) is defined by Wikipedia as "a phobia, when used in the context of clinical psychology, a type of anxiety disorder, usually defined as a persistent fear of an object or situation in which the sufferer commits to great lengths in avoiding, typically disproportional to the actual danger posed, often being recognized as irrational. In the event the phobia cannot be avoided entirely the sufferer will endure the situation or object with marked distress and significant interference in social or occupational activities."

Unhealthy or irrational fears are the reasons that you hold yourself back. They are the thoughts that stop you from moving forward to your positive goals, your Higher Self and your Inner Intelligence. It is that part of you that says "I can't." "I am not good enough." "I am not worthy." "I am not enough." "I will fail." "I am in danger." "I will embarrass myself." "I will get hurt". "I will not be accepted." "I have to be perfect." They are the voices inside your head that evoke terror, fear, anxiety, dread and self loathing. These are just thoughts. Thoughts can be changed. Notice where you place your attention. Is it on the negative or the positive? Do you see the glass of water half full or half empty? Do you want this thought to be creating your future? I think not!

Re-align your thinking by making a conscious effort to think positively. "Perception is the result of learning. Perception selects what you have chosen and makes the world you see. "The voice you choose to listen to in your mind and the visions that you choose to see reflect who you have decided you are.

We all have felt those thoughts. How we handle them in our day to day life makes all the difference in how much peace and joy we can allow ourselves to experience. I connected Love with God. Not the God who is a white, bearded male hanging out on a cloud waiting to condemn us all for failing not to sin. Nope, not him. I grew up with him. You know Onward Christian Soldiers? You don't have to see your God the way I see mine. Allow me to give you a good explanation of the God of my understanding: Unconditionally loving, unconditionally forgiving, unconditionally supportive; changeless - yet ever changing; formless - yet ever forming, creative energy; restoring energy, healing energy, abundance provider; nurturing energy; sustaining energy; Holy Spirit, Higher Power, Source of All; etc. There is no need for fear when I have a relationship with the God of my understanding! It is incredibly empowering to be loved so much!

In A Course in Miracles, Lesson 48 states "The presence of fear is a sure sign you are trusting in your own strength. There is NOTHING to fear." In my understanding this means that you must align yourself with some sense of a Higher Power/Inner Intelligence. It is not up to me to name YOUR understanding of God. I use the terms God, Holy Spirit or The Universe. I am not sure we could even come up with a word or series of words in our human condition to define such splendor, creativity, power and love. Honestly, I don't know how people who don't believe in something Bigger than themselves get through life. I have built, over time, a tremendous faith in Love or God or Higher Power or The Universe. For me, the name is not important. The intention, however, is critical.

To truly heal yourself you must get in touch with the Divine within you. That process provides you with incredible healing restorative power, unlimited possibilities and unconditional love. What is so scary about that? Most of it is scary in the beginning of your process and none of it is scary by the end of your process. It is hard to hear and feel your wonderfulness when someone else says it, if you are not yet able to see it within you. We tend to not accept it. We fight the compliments because we feel less than and not enough.

The transformation into accepting your own power has already begun. You have begun healing and restoring yourself as you have been reading this book. Knowledge is power. Now, work on releasing the past and forgiving everyone including yourself. The great Chinese philosopher, Lao-tzu said, "Someone must risk returning injury with kindness, or hostility will never return to goodwill." Start with loving yourself.

There are two mental patterns that contribute to disease: fear and anger. Anger can show up as impatience, retaliation, jealousy, irritation, hurt, frustration, pain, criticism, discouragement, resentment, or bitterness. These are all thoughts that poison the body. When we release this burden, all the organs in our body begin to function properly. Disease can be healed and health in body, mind and spirit can be restored.

Fear could be tension, terror, nightmares, anxiety, nervousness, worry, doubt, feeling uncomfortable, feeling insecure, night terrors, feeling not good enough or feeling unworthy. Do you relate to any of this information? You must learn to consciously substitute faith for fear if you want to heal. Faith in what? Faith in something bigger and stronger than we are: Love!

When we feel anger and fear and any of the uncomfortable feelings that come and go with those concepts we make ourselves sick. How do you think headaches, neck aches, stomach aches, ulcers, depression, strokes, heart disease, panic attacks and anxiety happen? They are truly heart aches internalized. Sadness and pain can create more dis ease than you can imagine. We are out of balance and need desperately to get back into balance. Hopefully, with the information in this book you will have the resources to begin your process and to move forward easily and successfully. Begin observing people you meet that show their anger or fear is a strong manner. They maintain being not at ease (dis-ease) and have many illnesses borne of this energy choice. Don't take other people's behavior personally. Just because they appear angry to you does not mean that they are angry at you.

Notice that you have some physical illness within you that is causing you to struggle. You see, you have been dealing with fear, anger and anxiety for so long you are not sure how to feel good. You know how to feel terrified. For some of us, in some incredibly dysfunctional way, feeling terrified actually feels somewhat comfortable because we are used to feeling it. Feeling good feels uncomfortable in the beginning. It is not what you have gotten comfortable feeling. It can be a bit stressful all on its own. I remember asking myself "how was I going to deal with this new energy of happiness, joy and excitement?" I used to only be aware of anxiety as a certain energy. When joyful excitement became a part of my life experience, I connected it to the adrenaline of fear. It felt so similar, but different. It does take time to reframe these responses. Don't be hard on yourself. In time, feeling good will be all you want to feel after you experience it regularly!

Chapter Three Workbook Exercise:

Name some illnesses you have had that you think were brought on by stress, fear or anger. Explain why you think this is true.

4

UNDERSTANDING WHO YOU ARE

It is critical for you to know who you are despite your current feelings about yourself. YOU are the LIGHT! YOU are a Child of the Universe! YOU are a Child of God! You are Love! Did I just hear the voice in your head say "NO, you are not!"? Yes, that is the voice of fear! That is the voice of the Ego. EGO has been said to mean Edging God Out or Evil Going On. Some people call that voice the devil or satan. It is amazing to what great lengths we battle with this negative energy. When you shine your light of love there is no room for the Ego, doubt or fear. Connect with the Love inside of you. If it takes a while to get there it is okay. Just keep practicing! It is learning to look from a perspective of non conflict.

Remember feelings are not facts. Truth resonates! There is a spark inside of you that no one can take from you. It is called by many names. Some call it the Soul, the Conscience, the Creator, the Source Energy, the Light, Holy Spirit, God or Goddess. I define it as a place where the The Divine resides within you. You have seen it and experienced it in others. You have seen it in pets. Have you ever looked into the eyes of a baby and seen that spark? You have seen it in people you love. That is it! It is also in You!

This is where Unconditional Love resides within you. You have a part of The Divine within you. You came into this life with Love in you. This is the place to tap when you are afraid, sad, anxious, fearful, depressed or grieving. It is also the place to tap when you are feeling your well being, love, joy, compassion, forgiveness, patience and peace.

You are not alone. Never. You may feel alone. That is an illusion. We are all One in the Great Cosmic Mystery. We all have life challenges, joys, fears, and moments of gratitude! There are Angels and Spirit Guides to help you along your journey. You may not believe this yet. I know from firsthand experience that this is true.

Visualization: How to tap being the LIGHT, you ask? Good question! Stop whatever you are doing. Calm your thoughts in your mind. Breathe deep a few times and go within yourself to the safe place where all happy thoughts abide. You can always think of a song you love to calm down. Think of something that makes you happy and vibrate your energy at a higher level than usual. Imagine the laughter of a child; the aroma of your favorite flower; the sounds of the ocean or a rippling creek.

Continue to turn off your thoughts. Keep breathing gently and deeply. Notice the sense of well being that you are feeling. You are in the present moment.

You are in the NOW. Your point of power is always going to be in the present moment. Not the past with its baggage or the future with its possibilities. Notice that as long as you stay in the moment you are feeling good, safe, and serene. Self- acceptance, self-approval and self love are major components of feeling empowered. Practice going deep within to this place as often as you want. In life, it really comes in handy if you can stop the chaos in your head and just go to a safe quiet space. For some, this is where meditation begins. For others, it is where inspiration pours forth. Everyone is different.

If it did not occur this time you didn't do anything wrong. You are not a failure. It is a process just like life. Remember when you were learning to ride a bike? You had to fall off a few times to get it right! Just like with the bike, get back up and try again! Practice makes perfect. Notice the thoughts that were running through your mind. They were fear thoughts. Resistance happens, even to the point of you starting to make a grocery list! They were fear thoughts. Resistance is fear. Who would you be if you were able to get to a peaceful space? What is the story that you have made up in your mind about you and about this process?

Chapter Four Workbook Exercise

It's all good. You can rest assured that you are Being the Light when you are unconditionally loving. Take time to time to write in your notebook about this experience. How did it feel? Were you afraid you wouldn't be able to get to the safe calm space? Did you get there? If not, what thoughts that you were thinking to stop this from happening?

5

WHAT STORY ARE YOU MAKING UP NOW?

A great teacher once asked me "What are you making up now?" in regard to a situation between us. I took that as an attack and became defensive. "I'm not making anything up!" I retorted. Yet, she was right. I was making up a story in my mind of how an event was going to play out. We all do it. We just do not necessarily know that we are doing it until it is pointed out to us.

Think back on your life so far. Ask yourself these questions: Did all the terrible situations you worried about actually come true? Did all the crises occur? Did all your fears blow out in one huge drama based crises? Of course they did not! Now, I will agree that some terrible things have happened. It happens to all of us. It is called Life. For most of us though, gratefully not all the terrible things we have worried about have come to pass.

Let's talk about the stories we make up. What I have noticed is almost all of them are fear based. We spend a lot of time creating fear based scenarios in our heads. Think about it. Some people do not sit around and make up happy, joyful scenarios in their head. It takes just as much energy to think of happy, fun and joyful scenarios than it does fear based thoughts.

When your teenager takes the car out to go to a party what do you think? Is it "she is well able to drive there and back and she will be safe?" Or is it "I hope she doesn't have an accident?" When your partner gets quieter and starts working late do you think she is having an affair? Or is she just tired and trying to make more money for the family?

Write down the first three fear based thoughts that you have in your head right now. Keep them handy. Later you will have the opportunity to get rid of them quickly!

The fear based stories we make up do not serve us. Yet we keep making them up until we don't. They are based on the Not Enough Syndrome. Do you know what that is? Here are examples: I am not skinny enough. I don't have enough money. I am not smart enough. I can't do it because I am not enough. I am not good enough. I will mess it up. I think I am crazy. I am not pretty enough. I am not handsome enough. I am too fat, too ugly, too thin or too poor. Fill in the blank.

Whatever the case may be in our mind - these are all lies and illusions. They are fear based thoughts. When we have anxiety it is because we have a big dose of not enough. We have bought into it to such a degree that we allow ourselves to be controlled by our fears and not our Inner Intelligence and the Love that is deep within us. We overspend to feel good enough. We attempt to keep up with the neighbors. We over compensate by over drinking, over eating, attempting to make ourselves believe that anything from the external material world might be able to make us feel good internally.

Our loving space would say to us: Yes you can! You will! I believe in you! I can do all things with God's help (however you see your God). I am well able! I am smart enough! I will do it well! I will survive! I am not crazy! I am competent. Watch me soar! I can make this happen!

We create the stories, in part, because we need a plan to live by. You know the "I am going to graduate from High School, go to college, get a great paying job, find the love of my life story? The one where; we are never going to argue with each other, we are going to have three kids who all are successful and have never encountered a problem. I am never going to have an emotional, financial, physical or spiritual challenge ever. It is all happily ever after story"! When you find someone who tells you that this is their life perhaps they are likely to have some swamp land in Florida to sell you too!

The stories we tell ourselves are important to know. If we do not become mindful of what we are telling ourselves we cannot change the message. First, you have to know what you are telling yourself. Then you have to have a way to be able to tell if the stories are real or made up. We are in charge of what we think. We have control over our thoughts.

It is important to observe what stories people claim for their lives. So many choose self-defeating thoughts. We have options. We could create a story that has us being healthy, wealthy and happy. Excuses play a big part of the stories. I can't do this because… I am never going to get what I want because… I will not be able to achieve this because… I cannot leave my house because I am afraid that… Fill in the blank. Where are the people who say "I am going to set this goal and make it happen"? They are near or at their goals! Where are the folks who say "I want to take chances and learn from life?" They are out creating an exciting adventure for themselves! We get the opportunity to choose what we want and go after it with wild abandon. I don't want to look back at the end of my life journey and say, "I wish I had done this or that" with regret. I want to be able to say, "Yes, I faced my fears with trepidation and when all was said and done I conquered them!" What do you want to say?

Chapter Five Workbook Exercise

Can you name some of the stories that you tell yourself? Name one story about your schooling or work. Name another about your relationships with others. Name a third about your goals and dreams.

6

THE WORK

A few years back, noted authors Byron Katie and Steven Mitchell wrote a book called **<u>Loving What Is</u>**. It is a phenomenal resource for folks to use to get clear about the stories they tell themselves. "The Work of Byron Katie is a way of identifying and questioning the thoughts that cause all the anger, fear, depression, addiction and violence in the world. Experience the happiness of undoing those thoughts through The Work, and allow your mind to return to its true, awakened, peaceful, creative nature. The Work is simply four questions that, when applied to a specific problem, enable you to see what is troubling you in an entirely different light. As Katie says, "It's not the problem that causes our suffering; it's our thinking about the problem."

Contrary to popular belief, trying to let go of a painful thought never works; instead, once we have done The Work, the thought lets go of us. At that point, we can truly love what is, just as it is." Byron Katie offers four questions to ask yourself about your thoughts.

Here are the four questions:

1. **Is it true?**
2. **Can you absolutely know that it's true?**
3. **How do you react, what happens, when you believe that thought?**
4. **Who would you be without the thought?**

Turn your thought around. Then find at least three specific, genuine examples of how each turnaround is true for you in this situation.

So let's try this. Go look at your list of three fears. I am going to use an example for the book.

My example thought is "I am too old to write this book."

1. No it is not true.
2. Yes I can absolutely know that it is not true.
3. When I believe this thought I am afraid to write my thoughts down for the book.
4. If I didn't believe this thought I might be selling lots of books and helping lots of people.

Turnaround: I can write the book.

It has the opportunity to become a bestseller!

I am not afraid to share my thoughts and experiences.

Let's try this again:

Thought: I will never lose weight so I better just get used to being fat.

1. Not true
2. Yes it is not true because I could lose weight. I wouldn't be fat.
3. I would feel so bad about myself. I would feel out of control, overweight, frustrated with myself, angry that I allowed myself to get into this situation and sad that I am not able to make the changes I think I want.
4. I would be more confident, probably weight less and like myself better.

Do the turnaround now.

Now let's look at this with **Anxiety:**

Thought: **I am not enough. If I don't hang out with this group of people I will just not be accepted.**

1. **Is it true?**
   NO!

2. **Can you absolutely know it is true?**
   No! I can absolutely know that this is not true.

3. **How do you react, what happens, when you believe that thought?**
   I feel less than, not good enough, unsure of myself, double checking everything I say and do, worrying all the time and stressed out.

4. **Who would you be without the thought?**
   More confident, less stressed out, happy, relaxed and peaceful.

You can use the four questions from Loving What Is *to get a reality check on your thinking anytime. It is best to practice using it until you know it by heart. Some people like to write the questions down in their cell phone or on a card to put in their pocket. Practice this process with a friend to make it more fun for you.*

7
THE UNSPOKEN RULES

I grew up in a family that had big expectations of me. In addition, it was a dysfunctional family structure with an active alcoholic/addict father and a co-dependent, but very loving, mother. There was no doubt that they loved me as much as they could, based on how much they understood themselves and loved themselves.

People cannot love someone else more than they love themselves. That is a myth. However, loving isn't enough. I learned many lessons at an early age. Some of them were:

* It is not safe when someone is drinking alcohol. Fights happen. Violence happens. Crazy stuff happens.

* It is not safe when someone is eating prescription pills by the pocket-full.

* It is not safe to trust others, even the ones who are supposed to love me the most.

* It is my responsibility to protect my drunken father.

* It is my responsibility to parent my father. He is sick and vulnerable.

* It is my job to make up excuses for why my father acts weird.

* It is my job to protect my mother from my father.

* If I cry and show I am afraid then I am not tough and might not survive.

* Don't make them mad or they will attack me.

* Walk on eggshells around everybody, keep them all happy with me and I will survive.

* Do whatever it takes to make them happy so there will be peace.

* My favorite is I have to be in control all the time to guarantee my safety and survival.

Now, I know that if you are reading this you might be saying, "Yes, I know that unspoken rule and this one too!" You might be having some memories all of a sudden from these words.

Write down your memories so you can use them later to reframe your thinking. Write down some of the unspoken rules from your childhood.

This flood of memories is called being "triggered" because the memories are triggered in you and you have to cope with them. Being triggered is not necessarily a bad thing although you may have associated some bad or sad feelings along with these memories. It is an opportunity to re-frame your thoughts and see them differently. Re-framing a thought means that you are going to take a look at that specific thought in a different way and see if you can change the thought pattern to a better more positive thought.

Millions of people have been brought up in broken, dysfunctional homes. We have learned certain coping choices that helped us when we were young to get through the tough times. The challenge becomes what do we do when the old coping strategies don't serve us like they used to in the old days? We have to create new coping strategies! This is a thought a way and with some practice can happen easier than you think. But, you have to practice it.

First, you have to become aware that your choice is not working for you any longer. Sometimes this happens easily, but, most often it is not until we have sabotaged ourselves and seriously hit bottom before we get it is not working. Here's where re-framing comes in. Creativity helps too. Tapping into your Healing Energy helps in a big way. Coming from a place of self love rather than self sabotage and/ or self loathing makes a huge difference in the outcome. Trust the process.

Take the four questions the Byron Katie shared in her book, <u>Loving What Is</u>. Ask yourself the questions for each thought that you want to rethink.

Intellectually knowing something is NOT the same as emotionally knowing something. It is clear to me, thirty years after the fact, that as an eight year old kid there was not much I could do to protect my mother from my father. There was nothing I could do to protect my father from himself. I tried because I felt it was my duty. The truth was that they were responsible for protecting me and they failed to do so at times. Children have a Magical Thinking mind that says they are responsible. We all have that little child still inside us. We have to love ourselves first and foremost.

We must learn how to do that to be able to get clear. We have to forgive ourselves. The Unspoken Rules were set in place to "protect" the dysfunctional family. We did not want our dirty little secrets put out for the whole entire town to know our business. Keep the secrets in the family. Don't think. Do what you are told. Don't question authority. Protect the family. Can you relate?

Chapter Seven Workbook Exercise

Take time out to write down some of your family secrets that you have held on to all these years. How could living in this environment cause you to be stressed? Fearful? Anxious? Depressed? What could you do differently NOW that you are in charge of your own thinking to reframe these thoughts? Are there any thoughts you can now discard and be free of? Write down which ones and why.

8
FEAR AND ANXIETY

What do anxiety attacks, panic attacks, panic disorder, generalized anxiety disorder and post traumatic stress disorder all have in common? **FEAR**. According to the National Institute of Health, "Anxiety Disorders affect about 40 million American adults age 18 years and older (about 18%) in a given year, causing them to be filled with fearfulness and uncertainty. Anxiety disorders last at least 6 months and can get worse if they are not treated. Anxiety disorders commonly occur along with other mental or physical illnesses, including alcohol or substance abuse and depression, which may mask anxiety symptoms or make them worse. In some cases, these other illnesses need to be treated before a person will respond to treatment for the anxiety disorder.

Anxiety is what happens when you take your mind out of the NOW Moment and attempt to go back into time dragging your painful baggage along with you or go forward into time and create something stressful in advance of the present moment. What story are you going to create for yourself? You and you alone get to make your choices and deal with the consequences of your choices.

There are certain physical responses when we are triggered to be afraid, anxious, fearful and stressed. Generally, your heart starts beating faster, your palms get sweaty, your thoughts are racing from one fear based thought to the next, the flight or fight mechanism kicks in with its adrenaline, and it seems like you cannot hear anything logical. You inherently know something is drastically wrong, but, you are not sure what it is or how to fix it. You are making up a story of how this disaster is going to go down.

You begin to feel totally out of control and you keep telling yourself those nasty stories built off fear based thoughts like I can't do it, I am a loser, I will fail, I am having a heart attack, I am going to die, I am nothing, and my personal favorite --I am going crazy. I am going to lose it all right here right now!

No wonder we scare ourselves to death. I used to have panic attacks about having panic attacks! I would feel anxious. I would bite my nails until they bled and bite them more. I would tell myself that the anxious feeling was a scary feeling (rather than perhaps an excited feeling). Then I would tell myself, "look… see your palms are sweaty, heart is racing you are out of control… totally out of control and you know, you could die of a heart attack if you are out of control! I would affirm that I was about to have a panic attack and that I was going crazy." Buddha said "We are the total sum of our thoughts." As you can imagine, I was a mess!

Generalized Anxiety Disorder, also known as GAD, is diagnosed when a person worries excessively about a variety of everyday problems for at least 6 months. People with GAD can't seem to get rid of their concerns, even though they usually realize that their anxiety is more intense than the situation warrants. They can't relax, don't sleep well, startle easily, and they have difficulty concentrating. Physical symptoms that often accompany the anxiety include fatigue, headaches, muscle tension, muscle aches, difficulty swallowing, trembling, twitching, irritability, sweating, nausea, lightheadedness, having to go to the bathroom frequently, feeling out of breath, and hot flashes. They anticipate disaster and are overly concerned about health issues, money, family problems, or difficulties at work. Sometimes just the thought of getting through the day produces anxiety. Now, we have all had some of these symptoms and have had a bad day here or there. You could read these symptoms and decide they describe a woman who is either pre-mense or peri-menopausal. This is different. This is daily.

"Generalized Anxiety Disorder affects about 6.8 million American adults, including twice as many women as men," according to the National Institute of Health The anxiety disorder develops gradually. It can begin at any point in the life cycle, although the years of highest risk are between childhood and middle age. Other anxiety disorders, depression, or substance abuse often accompany GAD, which rarely occurs alone. GAD is commonly treated with medication or cognitive-behavioral therapy, but co-occurring conditions must also be treated using the appropriate therapies. Do you see the pattern here that all of the stress based diseases can co -occur? It is more often than not, that you may have two of these dis-eases together: for examples anxiety attacks and depression or alcoholism and depression.

Treatment of Anxiety Disorders

Anxiety disorders are treated with medication, counseling, a spiritual transformation empowerment program or all of the above. Treatment choices depend on the problem, the person's preference and whether or not they have insurance. For those who do not have insurance, I encourage you to seek financial medical assistance and to pay strict attention to what I have been sharing with you. Your doctor needs to conduct a careful medical evaluation to determine whether your symptoms are caused by an anxiety disorder or a physical problem. If an anxiety disorder is diagnosed, the type of disorder or the combination of disorders that are present must be identified, as well as any coexisting conditions, such as depression or substance abuse. Sometimes alcoholism, depression, or other coexisting conditions have such a strong effect on you that treating the anxiety disorder must wait until the coexisting conditions are brought under control. You must be honest with your doctor. Tell them if you have symptoms of depression or alcoholism. Don't stay in your shame. Tell them the truth so you can get the help you need and deserve.

Medication will not cure anxiety disorders, but it can keep them under control while you receive counseling, go to treatment or learn to work a spiritual program to ease your stress and empower you to make healthier choices. Anti- depressants, anti-anxiety drugs, and beta-blockers are used to control some of the physical symptoms. With proper treatment and a spiritual program that teaches you to empower yourself you can get free from this prison in your mind.

Stress management techniques and meditation can help people with anxiety disorders calm themselves and may enhance the effects of counseling. Avoid caffeine and even some over-the-counter cold medications because they can aggravate the symptoms of anxiety disorders. Make sure to look at the ingredients on the cold medicine boxes. There are ingredients that will cause you to feel "speeded up". This will stress you out more. I have ignorantly done this to myself.

Panic attacks can occur at any time, even during sleep. I had a panic attack once in Key West. What a place to have a panic attack! Paradise! I was sleeping and the next thing I knew I was waking up my partner to call the ambulance. I thought I was dying! My heart was pumping hard. I could feel my blood pulsating into my fingers. I thought that I was dying. I was depressed at the time. The medics thought that I was having an allergic reaction to the shellfish from dinner. I took an embulance to the Emergency Room where I was treated by a doctor who did not have a great bedside manner. He didn't tell me it was a panic attack. He told me I was under too much stress and needed to relax. We had driven to Key West. I was in terror of it happening again in the car for the entire drive home. An attack usually peaks within 10 minutes, but some symptoms may last much longer. The dread and the fear last for days, weeks or months. Unfortunately, once we are in our fear it takes us time to choose to stop being afraid.

Panic disorder affects about 6 million American adults and is twice as common in women as men", according to the statistics provided by the National Institute of Health. Panic attacks often begin in late adolescence or early adulthood, but not everyone who experiences panic attacks will develop panic disorder. Many people have just one attack and never have another. Some researchers believe that the tendency to develop panic attacks appears to be inherited. Quite often people having a panic attack, just like with anxiety attacks, think they are dying or having a heart attack. Panic disorder is often accompanied by other serious problems, such as depression, drug abuse, alcoholism or mental illness.

"Post Traumatic Stress Disorder, also known as PTSD, affects about 7.7 million American adults," according to the National Institute of Health. It can occur at any age. Women are more likely to develop PTSD than men. There is some evidence that susceptibility to the disorder may run in alcoholic families. PTSD is often accompanied by depression, substance abuse, or one or more of the other anxiety disorders

Post-traumatic stress disorder (PTSD) develops after a terrifying ordeal that involved physical harm or the perceived threat of physical harm. The person who develops PTSD may have been the one who was harmed, the harm may have happened to a loved one, or the person may have witnessed a harmful event that happened to loved ones or strangers. For me it was waking up to a very emotionally deranged man yielding a very sharp hunting knife.

PTSD can result from a variety of traumatic incidents, such as rape, mugging, having been in a war, torture, being kidnapped, sexual abuse, child abuse, watching one parent harm another parent or child, car accidents, train wrecks, plane crashes, shootings, bombings, seeing violent actions on a loved one, or natural disasters such as floods or earthquakes.

Symptoms of PTSD are that they may startle easily, become emotionally numb pulling away from loved ones, isolating themselves from their peers, lose interest in things they used to enjoy, have trouble feeling affectionate, be irritable, become more aggressive, or even become violent. They avoid situations that remind them of the original incident, and anniversaries of the incident are often very difficult. Many folks in the New York area and the DC area now suffer from PTSD after the September 11th, 2001 World Trade Center attack. Most people with PTSD repeatedly relive the trauma in their thoughts during the day and in nightmares when they sleep. These are called flashbacks. Flashbacks may consist of images, sounds, smells, or feelings, and are often triggered by ordinary occurrences, such as a door slamming or a car backfiring on the street. A person having a flashback may lose touch with reality and believe that the traumatic incident is happening all over again.

I once went to a football bowl game with a friend who had suffered a loss in the World Trade Center attack. She was frightened by the fly over by the jets before the game started. It nearly ruined her game. Not every traumatized person develops full-blown or even minor PTSD. Symptoms usually begin within 3 months of the incident but occasionally emerge years afterward. They must last more than a month to be considered PTSD. Some people recover within 6 months, while others have symptoms that last much longer.

We had to trust ourselves when we were young and our caregivers were out of control due to their addictions or emotional unbalance. We learned quickly that if we didn't take care of us we could be in serious trouble. We learned to trust in ourselves. We created our stories early in our lives. Adult children of alcoholics and addicts are the best people to have around in an emergency. It is because they are so used to handling the crises that is in front of them that they shut off their needs and address the immediate needs. This starts very young. When all is handled and over then they go stress out.

Some of us just held that emotional release inside and really never let it out. We are the ones who have anxiety attacks and panic attacks. It appears to come out of nowhere. Yet it is coming out of somewhere… it is coming out of us! It builds up over time and without a healthy outlet our body says to us "there is something wrong here." Notice the problem now or it will come again and again and get stronger and stronger until you deal with it.

It eats at our psyche. You have been grocery shopping all your life. One day, you are going shopping and are at the store. All of a sudden, you think from out of nowhere, your heart starts beating faster and stronger, your hands become sweaty and your thoughts begin to race and seem to be flying through your mind faster and faster. You notice you are becoming frightened and are feeling out of control. You ask yourself where is this coming from and why? You feel something is wrong and you don't know how to stop it. You begin to look around to see if other people are noticing you because you feel out of touch with reality; you wonder if they can see you feeling weird. You feel you cannot trust yourself to be healthy. It feels like your body and mind are betraying you. You wonder why it is this is happening to you. It is a fearful place to be coming from no matter where you are standing. So you leave the groceries in the cart. Get out of the store and get to your car. You are running away from the geographical location. The problem is within you. You do whatever it takes to calm down. Many folks self medicate themselves with the hope that it won't happen again if they are medicated. Others call a friend. Still others go get an alcoholic drink to take the edge off.

Irrational fear eats at your insides to the point of physical symptoms like stomach aches, ulcers, headaches, high blood pressure and many more dis-eases. When you are not at ease with yourself you are dis-eased (not at ease). We make ourselves sick with our stories. We can make ourselves well with our stories just as easily. It is all in how you choose to think and hold your thoughts. Remember we tell ourselves these stories and then we continue to play them out until we don't. How long do you want to keep playing them out and suffering? In life, pain is inevitable. Suffering is optional.

If you are tired of being sick and tired you will choose to make a change in how you see the story you carry with such passion. Many people like being seen as the victim. Poor, pitiful victim…he is constantly in upheaval with such drama. In life, we get to choose how we are going to see each and every situation. You can choose to become bitter or better. Which attitude are you choosing? Create the life you really want not the story you keep playing over and over again in your mind based on old fear based thoughts.

Worry is a total waste of time. Let me explain this to you by asking you a question or two. Did worry ever serve you? Did your worrying ever help someone else? Doubtful the answer is anything but a resounding and loud NO! You get to choose to put your energy toward something every time. You can choose to stop worrying and transform that into positive energy toward the situation. You can claim your blessings and abundance in advance! Convert your worry into gratitude. It takes the same amount of energy but you feel better!

Can you take the same amount of time it has taken you to train your mind to think fear based and transform it into positive choices and positive thinking? Yes you can! It takes practice. We have unlimited amounts of opportunity each day to practice positive thinking and radical forgiveness. Forgiveness is powerful. Forgiveness frees us up. It is really not for the other guy. Forgiveness is for us. Begin the forgiveness journey by forgiving yourself first. At all times in your life you have done the best you knew how at that moment. Each day we learn new coping skills and new information. You cannot beat yourself up in your mind and expect your spirit to grow. It doesn't work that way. Holding on to anger and resentment are akin to drinking poison and expecting the enemy to die. It just doesn't work that way. Anger directed at yourself hurts you. It has been said that depression is anger turned inward. Resentment is based upon someone not meeting your expectations. Expectations breed resentment. Try not having expectations of everyone for an hour or for a day. It is challenging. However, you can change the way you see the world.

Chapter Eight Workbook Exercise

Name some people you want to forgive and why.

Name some people that you need to ask forgiveness from and why.

9
DEPRESSION

Depression is painful. No one healthy wants to be depressed. All the joy goes away. Fatigue and hopelessness set in. The desire for intimacy is depleted. You may either want to eat a lot or not at all. Sex is no longer desired. It is hard to face each day. You may ask yourself "What is the point?" You may cry often and it might seem like you can never blow your nose enough because you are congested due to the tears. You can't sleep or all you want to do is sleep. You may wake up and wish you were not starting the next day of your life. You may dread being alive for a time period. You may want to escape from life. You may feel like you are in some other world distantly away from everyone else. You may feel like all your thoughts are doom and gloom based thoughts. Some folks feel like they are deep down in some kind of black hole and the light at the end of that is a train coming at them full tilt. Most folks report feeling that no one will understand. It seems truly unreal compared with your normal everyday not depressed personality. You may isolate yourself away from friends and family because you just don't have within you what it takes to be around them temporarily. Sometimes, you don't even know you are depressed until you wake up one day and it hits you. Some folks drink alcohol so they can feel happy, to relieve the stress, sadness and fear; but it doesn't last long. Alcohol is a depressant. So you wake up the next day with less money, more depression and a hangover. Depression is not fun.

Major depressive disorder (MDD) (also known as recurrent depressive disorder, clinical depression, major depression, unipolar depression, or unipolar disorder) is a mental disorder characterized by an all-encompassing low mood accompanied by low self-esteem, and by loss of interest or pleasure in normally enjoyable activities "according to Wikipedia."

Symptoms of depression include:

* a significant change in your sleeping patterns

* a significant change in your sex drive

* a significant change in your eating patterns

* a sense of hopelessness

*inability to stay on task and focus for extended periods of time

*a noted loss in pleasure in normally enjoyable activities

* feeling like you want to die; also known as suicidal ideation.

I am not a medical doctor. I am in no way certified to offer you medical help on depression. I am not offering you medical advice here. I am sharing with you that I have fought depression for years. I have helped many folks who have had depression. I know how it manifests in me and in others. I can give you first hand experiences in handling depression. The first time I fought a bout of depression I was ten years old. I didn't know it was depression. I just remember vividly walking home from elementary school and feeling so sad that I just found a tree and sat down because I felt so hopeless and alone. I told myself I was so sad that I couldn't walk the rest of the way home without some downtime. (That was my story at ten.) I was a sensitive child in the middle of an ugly divorce. Everything I thought was true in my life was now distorted. My father was the be all to me. Everything he had taught me was turned upside down. My mother was barely holding it together because the man she had loved and sacrificed for over 23 years was choosing far too many unhealthy choices causing incredible heartbreak to us all. There I sat under the tree attempting to figure out how my life could be so messed up at ten. How was I supposed to cope with my heartbreak, my father's abandonment, emotionally, spiritually, financially and physically? I wondered how do I handle this incredible sense of loss and heartbreak without some help? How was I going to go on? As the darkness I felt creeping inside of me kept growing; so did the darkness that indicated the end of the day. I got up and walked home. I am a survivor. I moved on.

Sometimes we just ignore the symptoms of depression, or don't know the symptoms and keep pushing our bodies and minds to keep going. At some point, our cup overflows with stressors and it is obvious we need to get ourselves back in balance again.

I want you to know that if you feel depressed it is very important for you to get professional help. You need to go see both a medical doctor to get on some medicine to help the chemicals in your brain get back to balance and/or see a therapist to help you understand what is going on inside of you. When I say get your brain back in balance, picture this: in your brain are these neurotransmitters that bounce back and forth. They keep an even sequence back and forth when you are not depressed. When you are depressed, they don't go in the same rhythm. Envision a ping pong game where the players are evenly matched hitting the ball back and forth. This is similar to your brain neurotransmitters. Now, one of the players slams the ball across the table and off onto the floor. The sequence is completely off now and has to start again. This is a brain with a depression. The sequencing is off in the transfer of the neuro- transmitters.

Anti-depression and anti-anxiety medicine will probably be diagnosed with a starting dose and then adjusted as needed until you are feeling better. Then you stay on the meds until the doctor thinks it is time to reduce them and titrate off them. Usually this process is six months to a year. Don't decide to go off your medicine because you are feeling better. This is not wise. You and your doctor can decide together. Many folks start to feel better because of the anti-depression medication and therapy and just stop taking the medicine. Your depression can come back on you so quick that you won't realize how far deep down the black hole of depression you are until it feels that there is no way out. Don't set yourself up for a relapse!

There is no shame in being on anti-depressant and anti-anxiety medicines. Do not allow yourself to feel "less than" because you are depressed or anxious and getting yourself well! Would you feel the same way if you had broken your arm and had to go get it reset? Depression and anxiety are illnesses. Do not let other people attempt to tell you how you feel. Most likely, you are too numb or too sad to know until you have had some time for the medicine to kick in. Then talk with a licensed therapist or counselor if possible. I know that money can be tight. There are free counselors in most communities if you spend some time looking for them.

Chapter Nine Workbook Exercise

Name three symptoms of depression.

True or False:

1. *Depression only happens in adults.*
2. *Alcohol is not a depressant.*
3. *Get on anti-depressants and then choose to get off the meds when you feel better.*

10

DECREASING STRESS BY USING SELF-LOVE

When your anxiety is higher than normal your thoughts race around in your mind making you more stressed. The very first thing you have to do is work toward stopping the speed of the thoughts. They come so fast that it throws you off balance. You hardly have time to tell yourself "slow down" and the next thoughts are there. In addition, your body is physically starting to show signs of distress as I mentioned early on in the book. You have to take control of your thoughts and you can! Here are some suggestions to take into consideration to help you get you body in balance. This will help you become much calmer and feel better.

Breathing

I recommend changing breathing patterns. Try it for a few days. Breathe a deeper and calmer breath. Hyper ventilation may happen if you are panicking. Just attempt to get control of your breath. Slow your breathing down. With each breath say to yourself, "I am breathing out stress, and I am breathing in calmness." Keep this up until you start to get a sense of the stress backing off physically. Tell yourself "I can handle this reaction it is just a reaction." As you are able to sense more personal control you can tell yourself affirmations that will help you continue to get calmer. When physical symptoms continue tell yourself, "these are just symptoms of an anxiety attack.

I am not going to die or flip out. I am just going to breathe my way through this moment. I am going to be fine. I am fine now; I just haven't realized it yet." Remind yourself this is a trick of your mind and that you are taking charge. It becomes easier once you have been successful in talking yourself down. It gives you proof you can get through it on your own.

Reminder Messages

It takes practice. When you can feel like you are in control of your thoughts you begin your journey to empowerment. I suggest writing some thoughts down on an index card and putting them in your pocket or putting them into your cell phone. These thoughts are things to tell yourself when you are beginning to get anxious. Your thoughts are going to be different than someone else's thoughts. Your thoughts are for you and you alone. You can write new thoughts as needed. Read them to yourself when you are not stressed out so they will be known to you when you need to read them. Make an effort to connect a good feeling to the thoughts on the cards. This helped me quite often.

Creative Visualization

Use your imagination to help you rather than to imagine scary thoughts. Do you have a place in your mind you like to go to? Perhaps a warm sunny day by the water lying in a hammock feeling safe and calm? Maybe a magical cottage in the woods with flowers and your favorite animal or person nearby? If you don't have a safe space yet you can create one anytime and make all the details customized for you. You can't make it wrong because it is yours. You can add your favorite music in your safe space. Perhaps you are in a mountain cabin with friends and a fireplace. The major point is to go somewhere in your mind and create a sacred space where you feel at your very safest and best. The more you practice going to your scared space when you are not stressing the easier it is to go there when you are stressing.

Blood Sugar Issues

I struggled with blood sugar issues for years before I knew that was part of my challenge. Often, when I was having a blood sugar attack I thought it was an anxiety or panic attack. They have many symptoms that overlap. To ensure you are not having blood sugar issues I suggest you get a blood sugar test occasionally to see how you are handling carbohydrates and sugars in your diet. You may be telling yourself you are having anxiety attacks when, in truth, they are blood sugar issues. In the meantime, if you are feeling like an anxiety attack is coming on go drink a small glass of fruit juice. Do not go to chocolate or white refined sugar. Certainly, that will evoke a mood swing later in the day.

Caffeine

Avoid caffeine. Caffeine has the same symptoms of anxiety attacks when over consumed. How much is too much? Everyone is different with different body chemistry. No two people are going to respond the same way. If you love coffee, then, learn to love de-caffeinated coffee. You will find that you need time to titrate off of large amounts of strong coffee per day. One option is to drink one de-caf coffee each day in place of the regular coffee. Every couple of days, make adjustments to your daily intake adding more de-caf and decreasing the other coffee. Chocolate is the other most popular form of caffeine. Men and women with hormonal issues often eat chocolate to feel better. The question is about balance on this topic. Some chocolate will occasionally be ok to eat. However, to decrease anxiety when you are first learning how to transform your fears, stresses and anxiety into power just give it up for a few days. No doubt the holidays will arrive in time to tempt you to eat plenty of chocolate soon enough.

Sleep

It is clear that to feel better you need to have good sleep. Everyone's body is different. The average time for a recommended good sleep varies from six and a half hours to eight hours. You want to understand the emotions that rise up inside of you when you are overtired, anxiety rid and stressed. Make sure not to eat sugar or chocolate a couple of hours before you go to bed. I suggest that you do not drink caffeinated drinks for a few hours before bedtime. Another point to remember is not to overindulge in alcohol prior to going to sleep. This is even more important to know if you are on any kind on anti-anxiety or anti-depression drugs. Do not drink alcohol and take prescription medicine. It is an opportunity for a disaster.

Prayer and Meditation

According to Wikipedia, Prayer is "an invocation or act that seeks to activate a rapport with a deity or object of worship through deliberate communication. Prayer can be a form of religious practice, may be either individual or communal and take place in public or in private. It may involve the use of words or song. When language is used, prayer may take the form of a hymn, incantation, formal creed, or a spontaneous utterance in the praying person. There are different forms of prayer such as petitionary prayer, prayers of supplication, thanksgiving, and worship/praise. Prayer may be directed towards a deity, spirit, deceased person, or lofty idea, for the purpose of worshipping, requesting guidance, requesting assistance, confessing sins or to express one's thoughts and emotions". Dancing can be a prayer. Playing music can be a prayer. Drumming can be a prayer. Thus, people pray for many reasons such as personal benefit or for the sake of others. Prayer involves talking to God in a way that you feel comfortable. Praying to your Higher Power or to the God of your understanding heals and soothes the soul and spirit within you. Trusting that your prayers are heard and will be answered is very comforting. Gratitude is a form of prayer. Ritual prayers work for some people. Affirmations work for others. There is not a "right" way to pray. It is between you and your Source.

Meditation is a technique to quiet the mind. There is no limit to the ways of meditation. Every time we go deep within ourselves to our safe place we are meditating in some form. Each time we practice taking care of ourselves and controlling our thinking it gets easier than the time before. Each time we are able to quiet our mind, breathe deep and find relaxation or peace we are helping ourselves. Both terms involve slowing down our everyday thoughts and focusing on silence. Tapping the Spirit Within. Going into the depths of ourselves to tap the Source of Power that is larger than ourselves. Most of us have stared at a candle flame and "spaced out." That "spacing out" is the place where you want to get to with or without a candle flame. That place is a peaceful, calm, nurturing environment within us where insight and love can be felt and found. Other folks have used the term "sitting and staring". Different term, but same concept! Out of the immediate consciousness and into a place of calm and peace. You have actually been there many times but you did not realize it at the time. Meditation has been defined by Esther and Jerry Hicks in <u>The Law of Attraction</u> as "for 15 minutes each day, sit in a quiet room, wear comfortable clothing, and focus on your breathing. And as your mind wanders, and it will, just release the thought and focus back on your breathing."

Meditation quiets the endless chatter your mind offers you. You become the observer of your thoughts. You can become mindful of another state of consciousness. It is healing, soothing and comforting. It can renew your energy and restore your peace of mind. I encourage you to try it a few times to get the essence of it. Once you learn the skill set you will want to meditate often!

Hydration

Your body depends on water for survival. Did you know that water makes up more than half of your body weight? Every cell, tissue and organ in your body needs water to function correctly. Drinking plenty of clean water is a great way to keep yourself healthy. You lose water each day when you go to the bathroom, sweat, and even when you breathe. You lose water even faster when the weather is really hot, when you exercise, or if you have a fever. Vomiting and diarrhea can also lead to rapid fluid loss. If you don't replace the water you lose, you can become dehydrated.

De-hydration can make you feel anxious. Symptoms of dehydration include: dry mouth, sleepiness or fatigue, little or no urine, urine that is darker than normal, extreme thirst, headaches, confusion and feeling lightheaded,

It is more nutritious for your body and calmer on your mind to drink water than sugar loaded drinks. The white refined sugar in one brand name drink can crank your mood up, drop your mood down and bottom you out. Avoid high sugary high caffeine drinks if you are searching for balance. It has been suggested we drink up to eight glasses of clean, healthy water a day. Find your own balance with this one day at a time.

Exercise

Most of us do not exercise like we need to. I have found that it doesn't matter what your body type is you can do some exercise during the week. Start off with just a few minutes and build up your exercise plan. It will help you get your body in shape, your mind in shape and you will feel great about yourself too! If you are going into an anxiety attack, start running in place. It will change the energetic cycles you are creating. Your body will produce endorphins which will decrease your anxiety. Resist the temptation to just run away down the road in flight or fight moments.

Avoid Mind Altering Drugs and Alcohol

In our society, we are known for self medicating. Western medicine physicians write prescriptions for symptoms instead of teaching us how to deal appropriately with the root challenges. Alcohol intake is at an all new high. Drugs like marijuana, cocaine and crystal meth are popular, along with many other substances, based upon where you live and who you know. My personal experience was to self medicate my emotional pain, stuff it down deep inside of me and not deal with it. Getting high was all I did for many years. I cannot tell you I didn't have a good time. However, I can tell you I paid a huge price for it.

Numbing myself out of my emotional pain just made it fester and erupt in rage attacks, panic attacks, irrational fears, phobias, depression and unbearable sadness and grief. Not to mention drug withdrawal and how that affected my body and mind. I am here by Grace. Don't do this to yourself. It will come back to haunt you.

Eating Healthily

You have heard this all before I am sure. It bears repeating again. What you eat is fuel for your body and your mind. Your body will attempt to restore itself to balance. Choose healthy foods to fuel your body. Fresh vegetables and fresh fruits are essential to your diet and your nutrition. Reduce your white refined sugar intake and your moods will stabilize quicker. No one wants to hear this let alone do it. We grew up on sugar in everything. Proteins are great for you. Decrease your bad carbohydrates. You will begin to feel stronger and healthier if you begin this process and take it one day at a time making small changes here and there. Everything in balance!

Supplements

Many of us have deficits in some nutrients are body needs to be at its best. I have found that adding extra B vitamins to our diet helps with reducing the stress responses we have. B Vitamins are water soluble so your body takes what it needs and discards the rest. I feel that it is critically important to feed your body what it needs to function at your highest and best levels. The intention of taking back your power you have got to look at how your body is working and not working. There are thousands of supplements on the market. You have to research what you think is best for you. I use Monavie Nutritional products. I feel stronger and have a sense of well being when I use my Active Juice daily. I use the Elements Supplements, especially the brain and glucose elements, to make sure my body is receiving the nutrients it needs. You can get more information and order them from **www. jmannworldwide.mymonavie.com**

Music

Sometimes it helps to listen to music that comforts you when you are feeling anxious. I enjoy listening to Old School Rock, Blues, Jazz and Motown. It helps to soothe me. You may want another type of music. The point of this is that your mind is used to singing along with the music that you love. Connecting to the music re-frames the situation you are in. Singing comes from a place of love. It's is hard to stay in the fear based energy when your favorite music starts playing. These are simple coping options to help you get yourself centered.

Pick some music you love and set it up near where you sleep. Give yourself the gift of the music you love when you go to bed at night. Play the music you love before any stressful meeting or situations that you know in advance are going to be on your schedule. You will be amazed at how much more relaxed you are when you do this. Part of the reason you will be more relaxed is because you have been enjoying the music and not choosing to stress on a topic instead.

Take along your favorite music in the car if you are afraid of driving out of your comfort zone and need an extra gift of kindness for yourself. I was paralyzed with fear the first time I had to drive across the George Washington Bridge in New York City at rush hour. I started having anxiety about this drive for months before I had to go. I had myself all worked up. One night in prayer, it came to me that instead of stressing out for all the time before the trip I could plan ways to make it easier on myself instead. Imagine that!

So I created a CD with all my favorite happiness evoking tunes and had it in the car to use when I got into New Jersey. I made sure I had eaten healthily on the trip. I made sure I had slept well a couple of nights in a row before the trip. I had my best friends aware I might need to call them on my cell phone before I got on the bridge. I kept telling myself that thousands of people cross this bridge every day. I was well able to cross it without freaking out. I was going to like it once I gave myself the chance. I made it across without panicking! Then I felt so proud of myself! I noticed that right away my self esteem rose. I decided it wasn't that scary after all. Remember face your fear and it fades!

Alternative Healing Modalities

I encourage you to try some of these healing modalities. Have you ever had a therapeutic massage or some Reiki energy work? You must consider it if you have not. Massage can be one of the most healing choices you can make for yourself. Find a nationally licensed therapist who has experience in healing body work. Ask questions before you commit to a massage with someone you don't know. Find out where they went to school. Ask how long they have been practicing massage therapy. Ask if they are licensed. Tell them this is your first massage and that you want a Swedish or Stress Reduction Massage. Do not agree to a Neuro Muscular Massage, Pain Reduction Massage, Thai Massage or Sports Massage because they are not created for relaxation. They are excellent for their given goals. However, you want the first massage you get to be a relaxing pain free experience. When you lay your body down on the massage table, you can relax and let them work your body over in a healing and therapeutic manner. Make sure to drink 8 ounces or more of cold water when you are finished. This will help facilitate removing the excess toxins out of your body.

Reiki energy work can be a phenomenal healing experience if you open yourself to receive from the energy healer. Reiki energy work comes from Japan. It is painless. The healer uses their hands to send energy to various parts of your body by holding their hands over your body or on your body. You are clothed during this process. You can let go of being in control. You can let the energy flow through you and calm you.

Reflexology is where they work on your feet or hands in an intention to help facilitate healing by triggering specific trigger points on your body. This can feel great. It can be painful at times. Your body has been storing up all the energy from your emotions that are held within you. Your feet get a workout daily. Make sure to drink some good cold water when the reflexologist is finished their treatment.

Acupuncture is an alternative medicine methodology originating in ancient China that treats patients by manipulating thin, solid needles that have been inserted into acupuncture points in the skin. According to Traditional Chinese medicine, stimulating these points can correct imbalances in the flow of *qi* through channels known as meridians "Qi or chi" are words that mean life force or energy from within. Amazing medical changes have occurred with the use of acupuncture. I have found great relief for pain and stress with acupuncture. There are also great acupuncture treatments for those going through addiction withdrawal, panic attacks and depression.

Chapter Ten Workbook Exercise

Name three ways to decrease stress discussed in this chapter.

True or False: Anxiety attacks are similar to blood sugar attacks.

Name three symptoms of anxiety.

What can you tell yourself when you are beginning to have an anxiety or panic attack?

11

RESENTMENTS, GUILT AND BLAME

Resentment is a negative emotion that you experience when you feel you have been wronged in some way. This feeling of being harmed may be in response to an actual, real event or it may be imagined. In some cases your feelings will be irrational, but you won't be able to see that right away. Along with resentment comes anger, hatred and contempt. Contempt is felt when someone perceives that the person who wronged them is inferior. Anger is felt when someone is perceived to be an equal. Finally, hatred comes with the perception that someone is superior to the person being wronged. Remember this is all perception. The only one hurt by resentment is you.

Resentment is just another form of anger. Anger doesn't bring anything good into our lives. Resentment is a lack of acceptance and forgiveness. It is triggered in our own toxic minds, by the repeated thoughts of negative moments that have already happened. Holding onto resentment gives away the responsibility for that positive life experience, to whoever you are resentful towards and it causes stress and disharmony for a long time. Only you can control the feelings of resentment. You can choose your life experience. You can write your own story.

In their book _Ending our Resentments_, Ronald and Patricia Potter-Efron described the states of building resentment. "First, something angers or disappoints us and we do nothing about it.

We then start thinking all kinds of negative thoughts interpreting the situation that happened.

That is the first step towards losing trust in the person who we perceive as having wronged us.

All the while, we assume that person will read our minds and apologize. We progress through feeling like wanting to hurt that person in return. Resentments then grow firm when we 'see' a pattern. Blinded by our thoughts, we can now only see insults and slights. At this stage, even if an apology is given, it is too little, too late and all sorts of negative feelings start surfacing: hatred, revenge, feeling superior, etc. We might even decide to attack the person through vicious gossip, emotional or physical harm." Resentment is a major cause of relapse in recovery.

When you pause to consider the information the authors of Ending Our Resentments offer it rings true. Can you see yourself in this process? Where do you end up when this happens? How many times have you been in this position? We have all been guilty of these responses. The important point here is that we can move beyond them and come from a better and higher place.

I read this anonymous quote on resentment on a 12 Step recovery site awhile back and it sure made sense to me. "The moment you start to resent a person, you become their slave. They control your dreams, absorb your digestion, rob you of your peace of mind and goodwill, and take away the pleasure of your work. They ruin your religion and nullify your prayers. You cannot take a vacation without them going along. They destroy your freedom of mind and hound you wherever you go. There is no way to escape the person you resent. They are with you when you are awake. They invade your privacy when you sleep. They are close beside you when you drive your car and when you are on the job. You can never have efficiency or happiness. They influence even the tone of your voice. They require you to take medicine for indigestion, headaches, and loss of energy. They even steal your last moment of consciousness before you go to sleep. So—if you want to be a slave—harbor your resentments!"

Harboring resentments makes you sick in body, mind and spirit. If you want to feel great, you have to choose to allow your resentments to go away. See yourself carrying around this large bag of rocks. Each rock is equal to one resentment. How many rocks are in your bag? Are you able to see that each resentment you release can be removed from the bag? It weighs a ton. The bag is hard to carry around. It causes you pain. Get rid of the resentments and the pain will cease.

The first step in releasing resentment is to be willing to feel your pain. Look under the resentment and find the pain. Find the feelings of being not good enough or not worthy enough that you are avoiding. One way to release your resentments is to write a letter to the person you are resentful toward. Write down all the specific injustices that you feel whether they are real or percieved. Write down all the negative impacts that it has had on your life. Then at the end write this statement: "but I choose to forgive you and move forward". Do not send the letter. Now you have two choices. You can tear it up into tiny pieces and throw it away or you can take it to a safe place and burn it up. Allow yourself to let those resentments go away. Allow yourself to be at peace.

Take time to write down your top resentments in your notebook. Take time to look at them and see if you can find a new way to look at them. Write it down to review later.

In the 12 Step Recovery Community there are many life changing teachings on resentment. I encourage any of you who have a desire to get free of your addictions to go to a 12 Step recovery meeting.

How many times have you gotten yourself all worked up over something small that blew up into something bigger because you sat on it until it festered? I am confident that resentments can create chaos, drama and lack of serenity. Lots of worry and fear will go away if you just let go of your resentments. The need to be right has to be lessened in an argument. Step back and reflect how you can de-escalate the argument while carrying on a loving conversation. Don't take what people say to you personally. Don't take it personal when they act poorly. It's all about them. Not you! Move out of the line of fire by realizing it doesn't matter what others say or do. The truth always wins out over time. Just be you with all the love you have to share and ignore others who don't resonate with your energy. Like attracts like. If you send out loving energy then loving energy will soon be coming back to you. Have you heard the term "projection"? Projection can be defined as a defense mechanism where the person arguing with you projects their poor sense of self back on to you.

They may say "you are a jerk". What they really mean is "I am feeling like a jerk but can't admit it so I'll call you a jerk instead." They might say "You are selfish". What they really mean is "I am selfish." Be careful when you hear terms like "never" and "always" in arguments. These are a red flag something is probably amiss.

Guilt

When you have guilt, you reinforce the feelings of being not okay. You lose your confidence and your self-respect. You feel undeserving of love. You hold yourself back. You beat yourself up with negative self talk. The key to letting guilt go is to recognize that you go through life doing the best you can with the limited skills that you have at the time. If you knew differently then you would have chosen a different choice.

Unfortunately, the life skills that you have are rarely enough. This results in you making mistakes. Making mistakes is part of the human process. This is how you learn. Every time you make a mistake you learn a little more about how to choose differently. Ten years from now you will be much wiser than now. The wisdom you will have learned in ten years from now doesn't do you any good today. The wisdom and life skills that you have today didn't do you any good back when you made your mistakes. This is true because back then, you didn't know what you know today. You only knew what you knew. Forgive yourself. Forgive yourself for not being smarter and more intentional. Forgive yourself for the damage that you caused as a result of your lack of awareness.

Blame

Blame happens when you don't want to have to look at yourself and your actions. If you looked at yourself, you would have to experience all the hurt from what happened. You would have to feel all the hurt of being not good enough and the pain of feeling not worthy of loving. So you put your negative attention on someone else so you won't have to look at yourself. Blame is a clever way for you to divert your attention from what is real and needs attention. It allows you a temporary escape route and a means of avoiding the truth. The truth is always something too painful for you to readily accept, or something that you feel is out of your hands, or that you have no hope of resolving. However, the truith does win out. Responsibility and accountability for your actions and your feelings will make you much more empowered than hiding behind an excuse! Decide today to take your personal power back from your excuses.

Chapter Eleven Workbook Exercise

Take a moment to reflect on your resentments that you wrote down earlier. Do you still have any resentments that you have not reconciled in some way. Write them. Share them with someone who supports you emotionally.

12
FORGIVENESS

Forgiveness heals. It is only when we have completely forgiven others that we can get clear in our own minds. Holding grudges is hazardous to our health. When we are criticizing and condemning others we hold that energy within ourselves. It occupies our thinking and poisons it. When we feel we have been injured it is normal to want to strike back out on the person we believed has harmed us. No one wins in that battle. The one up game causes more destruction. Forgiveness is for you. When you hold the energy of anger and hatred within you it will make you sick. Forgiveness is both for others and for yourself. We must learn to forgive ourselves. It is part of the self love process.

Forgiveness asks us to admit that we did not come close to our expectation of what we thought we needed to do or that someone else did not measure up to our expectations of them. It asks us to be gentle with ourselves and with others.

Forgiveness reminds us that we have made our fair share of mistakes. If we do not forgive daily, the resentments will challenge our thought processes and we will not be at peace. You may not be able to forgive someone forever today. But, you can forgive them for today. Your peace of mind requires it.

Forgiveness asks us to be compassionate with ourselves and others. It does not mean that if someone harms us that we are agreeing that it is acceptable to harm us. It is us saying you made a mistake. I know you were doing the best you could at the time. I will learn to have healthy boundaries. I will not allow you to harm me again in that manner. I will not hold your mistake against you. I will not hold my mistake against me. Basically, it is saying it is what it is. Let us move forward.

Forgiveness allows us to make our mistakes and forgive ourselves when we acknowledge that others make mistakes as well. When we are able to forgive others we find that we are also able to forgive ourselves. We are able to love ourselves more when we can accept our own mistakes and shortcomings. Making amends for our mistakes need to be addressed at that point. We must let go of old patterns, old wounds and old grudges if we want to move forward in our life. Letting the old ways go and choosing to be intentional on being the best you can be in the present moment. Perhaps they were doing the best they knew how to do at the same time you were doing the best you knew how to do. Whatever anyone did that you perceive is an attack against you is most likely all about them and how they see themselves and has little to nothing to do with you in truth. People project their fears, anxiety and judgments onto us as a defense mechanism. What someone says or does in reference to someone else is a direct response to how they feel about themselves. We just take it personally when, in truth, it is not personal. But it sure feels personal!

There is a school of thought in A Course in Miracles that holds that forgiveness is for what we don't do as well as what we do act on. This theory holds that we have decided that we were not harmed by someone else. We were harmed by our perception of what someone did to us. Forgiveness could be the process of joining with another person who had been perceived to be separate from us. In truth they were not separate. Ultimately, We are One.

Chapter Twelve Workbook Exercises

Make a list of those people you feel you choose to forgive to move forward. Find a quiet place to focus. Say to yourself "I forgive you,_____, for _____I release you and myself from this negative energy. Go in Peace and Love."

13
GRATITUDE

Gratitude is an incredibly strong positive energy. The more you practice gratitude the stronger and more profound your gratitude will feel. It is one of the most powerful energies in the Universe. Saying "thank you" to God, The Universe, people or pets in your life is always a good feeling. Start practicing when you get up in the morning. Name some things to be thankful for as you begin your day, as you are driving to work, during the day and at bedtime. There is no time or place where it is wrong to be thankful. It raises your own energetic vibration which in turn, decreases your anxiety and stress. In addition, once you have had some practice with gratitude you begin to become aware of how your energy changes and the lighter and less stressed you feel. Your mind notes that and learns to move toward that happy place with a higher energetic vibration rather than toward your fear based thoughts. It is up to you to learn how to control your mind. It is easier to do than you think if you practice when you are not in as stressful situation. You become more mindful of the environment around you and how you interact with that environment.

Gratitude allows you to become aware of just how abundant your life is in the Now Moment. It is easy to become complacent in remembering how wonderful we have it compared to others in blessed when gratitude is expressed. Demonstrating sincere gratitude takes energy and thought. Having an attitude of gratitude requires the conscious effort of being thankful. It is easy to be grateful when things are going well in your life. What about when you have gotten fired, or your relationship has broken down or you are angry? That is when gratitude has to come from a deep within spiritual place. It is the same way as when we are forgiving someone. It is easy to forgive some things and people. When we have to dig deep within and grow to forgive others is when the real work begins. An awakening of the spirit within is one of the greatest gifts we can receive.

People who model gratitude don't take others for granted. They don't make assumptions about how other people should treat them or what others should do for them. They don't walk around with a sense of entitlement, feeling they are owed more from the world. They dont get resentful easily. One of the best things you can do for yourself is to create an Attitude of Gratitude. Find the good in every situation. Make that your intention and practice everyday. Meister Eckhart, a German theologian from the 13th century, wrote: "If the only prayer you said your whole life was 'thank you' that would suffice."

Chapter Thirteen Workbook Exercise

Creating a Gratitude Journal will help you begin finding situations in which to be grateful. Start each day by writing down a few things in your Gratitude Journal See how many different things you can be grateful for in the first week, month and year. You will be amazed at the miracles that begin to show up in your life!

14

THE UNIVERSAL TEACHINGS – THE WAY

Transformation comes from being awakened. There is a story about Siddharta Gautama, the historical Buddha. He was walking down the road when he met a fellow traveler. The traveler perceived a great radiance emanating from Siddaharta. Instead of asking "Who are you?" he asked "Are you a god or a divine being?" "No", answered the Buddha. "Are you a shaman or a sorcerer?" "No," answered the Buddha. "Are you a man?" Again the Buddha answered, "No." "Well then, the traveler said, "what are you?" The Buddha answered, "I am awake." How did he awaken? He went within. He calmed himself. He walked his path on his journey just like you are doing now.

Jesus, according to the Gospels of the New Testament, was victorious over all temptations from Satan. It has been written that everywhere he went, people quit what they were doing to follow him because those who met him knew he was no ordinary man. He emanated love energy. He had wisdom others did not have. He had Knowledge from within. Jesus taught loving, kindness and forgiveness. He taught mercy and understanding. He taught about a God of Love rather than a God of Fear. Whether you are a student of Christianity's teachings or not, you can see how these teachings could only increase love. The quotes "The Kingdom is within you" (In other words, deep within you is the Source of All, Love, God Within.) and "Love your enemies" were attributed to Jesus. The inference is you must love yourself before you can love your enemies. "Jesus taught that people just needed to perceive reality with new eyes. If they could alter their perception, they would see that God was everywhere, most especially within themselves." This is according to Richard Hooper who edited <u>The Parallel Sayings</u>. This God that is within you can be called many names including Inner Intelligence, The Universe, Holy Spirit, the Divine. Creative Energy and many more. Unfortunately, so many people get caught up in having the name that they feel is "right" and or what they have been taught is "right" to be the only name of God. It is far more important to get the truth lesson than to argue over the name of the Source.

Here are but a few of the teachings attributed to Lao Tzu in the <u>Tao Te Ching</u>

"Be careful what you water your dreams with. Water them with worry and fear and you will produce weeds that choke the life from your dream. Water them with optimism and solutions and you will cultivate success. Always be on the lookout for ways to turn a problem into an opportunity for success. Always be on the lookout for ways to nurture your dream."

"Watch your thoughts; they become words. Watch your words; they become actions. Watch your actions; they become habit. Watch your habits; they become character. Watch your character; it becomes your destiny."

"Being deeply loved by someone gives you strength, while loving someone deeply gives you courage."

"Kindness in words creates confidence. Kindness in thinking creates profoundness. Kindness in giving creates love."

"Because of a great love, one is courageous."

"Love is of all passions the strongest, for it attacks simultaneously the head, the heart and the senses."

The words of Krishna in the <u>Bagavad Gita:</u> "The most precious gift we can offer others is our presence. When mindfulness embraces those we love, they will bloom like flowers."

"Man is made by his belief. As he believes, so he is."

"Still your mind in me, still yourself in me, and without a doubt you shall be united with me, Lord of Love, dwelling in your heart."

"On this path effort never goes to waste, and there is no failure. Even a little effort toward spiritual awareness will protect you from the greatest fear."

Both Krishna and Lao Tzu taught that attachment to that which is impermanent causes suffering. Give up attachment and suffering ceases. Consider this: your attachment may be to your story that you have made up about yourself. Give up your old story and your suffering ceases. It is time to change your story?

Paramahansa Yogananda said ""The habit of being inwardly in the calm presence of God must be developed, so that day and night that consciousness will remain steadfast. It is worth the effort, for to live in the consciousness of God is to be done with enslavement to disease, suffering, and fear."

"Forget the past, for it is gone from your domain! Forget the future, for it is beyond your reach! Control the present! Live supremely well now! This is the way of the wise…"

"Be afraid of nothing. Hating none, giving love to all, feeling the love of God, seeing God's presence in everyone, and having but one desire - for God's constant presence in the temple of your consciousness - that is the way to live in this world."

If you gave up your story, who would you be and what would it look like?

Could you not create a more self loving story with a happier ending?

The Way is the journey within you to come to peace and to still anxiety and fear. The Way is a route to learn how to never have to deal with a panic attack or fear. The Way is not a religion. It is a journey, a path, a way to be free of stress. The Way does not have to cause you distress with regard to your religious upbringing. Truth resonates. I urge you not to ignore this section as it can provide you with great knowledge if you let go of your religious challenges and just go with the flow.

Buddha said in <u>The Dhammapada</u> "Looking within, finding stillness - free from fear, free from attachment - know the sweet joy of the Way." "Those who meditate and keep their senses under control are able to do always what ought to be done… and so their suffering ceases."

Suffering for me was a full blown panic attack. It was my definition of hell. I was absolutely motivated to find out how to not have them. If The Way included helping me learn how not to have them I was in for the ride! I tip toed into each area we have discussed. I wanted to know more as I felt safer and learned to trust the process. Did I have some incredible stressed out moments on my journey so far? Yes! I would fall back to using old coping skills that didn't work for me anymore. I had to remind myself of it often. I made a decision that whatever I was thinking before was not working any longer. It might be scary to learn new thoughts and information but it was sheer terror to live in my fear. Suffering motivated me to try something different. Does it motivate you? Can you make a commitment to yourself to be the best person you know how to be in each moment?

I am not promoting religion here. Let me be perfectly clear. More people have died in the name of religion than I can begin to write about. I am talking spirituality; going within, creating a connection with the Divine, loving yourself and loving others. Seeking peace, which includes not stressing out, worrying, and doubting. Knowing what you are feeling and becoming aware of how you respond and react internally. Reacting comes from fear. Responding comes from thinking things through from a personal point of power.

I had to learn to not speak poorly about myself to myself and to others. Self-loathing to self loving is a journey you can make and will want to make the more you start believing in yourself. Learning to surrender to the process. Walking your path to a peaceful place internally where you can take in the day and not get upset. What would that look like for you?

Here is a hint: Do not go to a well that is dry if you are thirsty. Take a look at your patterns of behavior. Where do you go when you need some positive energy added into your life? If you are going to places that in the past may have helped, know they may not help any longer. They made make it harder. I would repeatedly go back to situations and people who did not have the skill sets to help me through my journey. I might as well have been hitting my head against the concrete wall. When you need direction, go to someone who has some experience with successfully achieving positive goals. Do not go to someone who has an opinion, but, has not walked in your shoes. You can always go within and tap into the Inner Intelligence inside of you.

Write in your notebook about what a stress free day would look and feel like for you. Remember to add as many details as you can! The aroma of the roses, the smell of a fresh cup of coffee, a warm genuine hug are all details. Now, take your time and visualize it.

It is hard to imagine a whole day of no stress right now in your life. That will change as you begin to walk your journey trusting the Universe will guide you gently. Each day will be a new adventure that you will be able to use your new thoughts you choose to think, your gratitude skills and your ability to be self - loving. Choose not to hold beliefs that are not in harmony with your true desires.

In The Law of Attraction, authors Jerry and Esther Hicks via Abraham share that "The more attention/energy you give to a topic the more powerful it becomes; the easier it is to think about it and the more it begins to appear in your experience." This can happen both positively and negatively. Remember earlier in the book, I shared with you that I would talk myself into panic attacks about thinking I was going to have a panic attack? That is definitely focusing on the negative. Stop that if you are doing that! Farther along in the book, I share with you about affirmations and how they work. That is a positive focus and one I encourage you to use daily. The more you tell yourself how great you truly are the more you will learn to believe your thoughts and trust them to be true. Your confidence will grow. You will be making decisions from your own personal point of power!

Chapter Fourteen Workshop Exercise

Can you name three things that you would like to manifest into your life by focusing on positive rather than negative? Do that now.

15

AFFIRMATIONS

Affirmations are sentences that tell us something positive or negative about ourselves. You are declaring a thought into your life. Words have tremendous power. Always state your affirmations in the present tense. Start them out with "I am…" or "I have…" It can be something that is currently true and it can be something you are speaking into existence for your future. Your subconscious mind doesn't know the difference from the truth and what you say. Dr. Bernie Siegel, author of <u>Love, Medicine and Miracles</u> wrote that "affirmations are not a denial of the present, but a hope for the future. As you allow them to permeate your consciousness, they will become more and more believable until eventually, they become real for you. "Writing an affirmation makes it more powerful for you. Choose thoughts that nurture and support yourself.

Here are some affirmations that may be helpful to you. Read them aloud and see how they feel for you.

Some will feel stronger or resonate energetically with you than others:

I am always safe wherever I go.

I am brave.

I am willing to change.

I am always protected.

I have all I need for today.

I am loved.

I love and accept myself.

I am forgiving.

I am open to recieve from places known and unknown.

All is well in my world.

I am the source of my happiness.

I am compassionate.

I deserve to feel loved.

I am kind.

Loving myself and others gets easier every day.

I am brave.

I am perfect just as I am.

I am calm.

My healing is already in process.

I deserve inner peace and accept it now.

My mind is strong and clear.

I trust my intuition.

I am worthy of love.

I am trusting the Universe.

I am at peace.

I have abundance in my life.

I am free from stress.

I trust my inner wisdom to guide me.

I know that God is working!

This is my favorite affirmation. It comes out of A Course in Miracles, Workbook for Students, Lesson 34 "I can see peace instead of this." (You define what the "this" is.) This could be a problem, challenge, feeling, situation, argument, fear, anxiety, stress, terror or other negative emotion.

It has been a considerable help to me as I reframed my world. I transformed my fears into a new thought process. It helped me become empowered enough not to have those same stressors eat at my peace of mind again. "Peace of mind is clearly an internal matter. It must begin with your own internal thoughts and move outward. It is from your peace of mind that a perception of a peaceful world arises." ACIM Lesson 34, 1:2

Chapter Fifteen Workbook Exercise

Can you add some affirmations in your notebook too?

16

ADDICTIVE BEHAVIOR

You cannot imagine how many people struggle with addictive behavior. The root thought in addictive behavior is "I am not enough". We don't want to feel our feelings. We hurt. We ache. We grieve. We wish we were different. We don't want to feel the pain so we self medicate. How do we self medicate? Drugs, alcohol, food, debt, gambling, sex, shopping, sugar and anything that will numb us and distract us from our pain.

Some of us have addictive personalities and once we start using our drug of choice we can't stop without support, a spiritual awakening and changes in thinking. We will lie, cheat, steal, trade sex, give up our integrity, and do anything that will keep us from feeling and feed our addiction. More than anything we share a self hatred. We don't know how to forgive ourselves. We punish ourselves. We are fearful. The idea of letting go and trusting the process is terrifying. Our story is that the world is an unsafe place. Many of us have struggled with abuse in early childhood: sexual abuse, alcohol abuse, drug abuse, physical abuse, emotional abuse, emotional incest- all from people who we were told were here to keep us safe. The emotional turmoil of guilt, shame, remorse, self hatred, self loathing and realistic fear, and irrational fear all add up to a major head game.

Deep inside of us is this little child yearning to be safe and loved. Addicts can be the most charismatic people with the deepest seated pain. Most of us learned early on that we needed to be in control to keep ourselves safe from the dangers in our environment. We have known abandonment like no other. We have seen what out of control looks like. We have learned to manipulate the variables to get what we think we need. Compulsive behavior is how we have learned to survive our pain. Our addictive personalities are fear based and understandably so. To start healing the addictive cycle we must become aware that we have a problem. Most of the time that is not so easy to admit. Denial is more than a river in Egypt. It is a defense mechanism that tells us that we do not have a problem. It rationalizes our actions and attempts to convince us we are alright. We have told lies so long we often cannot distinguish the truth. We have to want to change. Some folks are much more comfortable in their dysfunction than in creating change. Change is scary. Dysfunction is a known situation. The outcomes are predictable. We would have to feel our feelings to change. Feelings like self-hatred, insecurity, self-loathing, anger, pain, grief, and the dreaded vulnerability need to be felt. It is not comfortable. It can be done though. The more that we feel our feelings and deal with those feelings the less powerful and scary they become.

The challenge in addictive behavior is that we have used external things to attempt to create internal peace. This does not work. For addicts, it is even tougher because we create our stories that we need our compulsive addictions to live. Going for one hour without a drink may be so terrorizing that we drink twice as much just at the thought. Liquid courage is what it is called. It just doesn't work. Deep underneath all that facade is a wounded person struggling.

The stories we make up are the ones we live out. You have an opportunity in every moment to begin to make the necessary changes to get clean and sober. One of the best routes and one of the least expensive routes is to join 12 Step Recovery groups. I have learned much in the rooms. It is a safe place to land, begin your process, get a sponsor and make some new friends who genuinely care about you and your well being. Meetings are free, but if you have a dollar or two, you can toss it in the basket when it comes around to help with the overhead. The only requirement is a desire to quit using your drug of choice.

Here is a partial list of some of the 12 Step recovery groups in the USA and internationally. They are worldwide so if you are outside the USA just go to your computer browser and type in the key words.

Alcoholic Anonymous	www.aa.org
Narcotics Anonymous	www.na.org
Overeaters Anonymous	www.oa.org
Debtors Anonymous	www.debtorsanonymous.org
Gamblers Anonymous	www.gamblersanonymous.org
Sex and Love Addicts Anonymous	www.slaafws.org
Cocaine Anonymous	www.cocaineanonymous.org
Ala-non Family Groups	www.alanon.org

There are two mental patterns that contribute to dis-ease: fear and anger. According to Marianne Williamson, "Anger is one of fears most potent faces." It keeps us from receiving love when we need it the most. I know we need to be in touch with our anger and release it in a healthy manner. Anger can show up as impatience, retaliation, jealousy, irritation, hurt, frustration, pain, criticism, discouragement, resentment, or bitterness. These are all thoughts poison the body. When we release this burden, all the organs in our body begin to function properly. We become less dis-eased. We begin the process of inner healing.

When we are afraid, we need to be able to express our fear. Unfortunately, what we usually do is convert our fear to anger because it feels easier to handle energetically. It is important to be able to be afraid and ackowledge that you are dealing with fear. Fear could be tension, terror, nightmares, anxiety, nervousness, worry, doubt feeling uncomfortable, feeling insecure, night terrors, feeling not good enough or feeling unworthy. Do you relate to any of this information? You must learn to substitute faith for fear if you want to heal. Faith in what? Faith in something bigger and stronger than we are: Love!

When we feel anger and fear and any of the uncomfortable feelings that come and go with those concepts we make ourselves sick. How do you think headaches, neck aches, stomach aches, ulcers, depression, strokes, heart disease, panic attacks and anxiety happen? We are out of balance and need desperately to get back into balance.

The more consistently you work a spiritual program of transformation the quicker you will heal yourself. Hopefully, with the information in this book you will have the resources to begin your process and to move forward easily and successfully.

Here is a copy of the Twelve Steps of Alcoholics Anonymous for those who are dealing with active addiction or are interested in this program. Change the word in line one where it says "alcohol" if your addiction is drugs, food, gambling, sex, overeating or other issues besides alcohol.

THE TWELVE STEPS OF ALCOHOLICS ANONYMOUS

1. We admitted we were powerless over alcohol—that our lives had become unmanageable.
2. Came to believe that a Power greater than ourselves could restore us to sanity.
3. Made a decision to turn our will and our lives over to the care of God as we understood God.
4. Made a searching and fearless moral inventory of ourselves.
5. Admitted to God, to ourselves, and to another human being the exact nature of our wrongs.
6. Were entirely ready to have God remove all these defects of character.
7. Humbly asked Him to remove our shortcomings.
8. Made a list of all persons we had harmed, and became willing to make amends to them all.

9. Made direct amends to such people wherever possible, except when to do so would injure them or others.

10. Continued to take personal inventory and when we were wrong promptly admitted it.

11. Sought through prayer and meditation to improve our conscious contact with God, as we understood God, praying only for knowledge of His will for us and the power to carry that out.

12. Having had a spiritual awakening as the result of these Steps, we tried to carry this message to alcoholics, and to practice these principles in all our affairs.

Copyright A.A. World Services, Inc.

As you can see, they have created a program that uses many of the ideas that are in this book. There is decision to allow changes to occur, making a decision to improve conscious contact with God as we understood God, being open to change, making amends, prayer and meditation, dealing with our feelings and helping other people.

Addiction is a disease. Anxiety, Irrational fear, and Panic Disorder are diseases. It is clear to me that when we are not at ease (dis-eased) with ourselves we are out of balance. When we are out of balance we make decisions that may not be in our best and highest good. Alcoholics Anonymous has had the greatest success of any group or plan to help beat alcoholism.

Chapter Sixteen Workshop Exercise

What is the very first thing we have to do to know we have an addiction problem?

Where can we go if we have an addiction issue?

True or False

1. *Alcoholics can't quit drinking. T or F*
2. *12 Step recovery groups are expensive. T or F*
3. *Most addicts hate themselves. T or F*

17
TRUST

Trust takes a significant time to create and seconds to destroy. What exactly is trust?

According to Merriam Webster Dictionary, "Trust is a reliance on the integrity, strength, ability, surety, etc., of a person or thing; confidence; confident expectation of something; hope; a person on whom or thing on which one relies. *God is my trust.*"

In a healthy family structure, trust is part of a foundation that is built for us to grow, develop and become healthier. We could trust our parents, extended family, caregivers, and selected friends and community leaders. Unfortunately, all too often that has not been the case. In reality, we were taught to trust certain people. They had our trust and they broke our trust by making choices that were not in our best interest. It is a healthy response not to be too trusting of other people if your own parents or your family have broken your trust.

Those of us who have suffered and continue to suffer with anxiety disorder and panic attacks have often had their trust irretrievably broken. I have found working with people over the past thirty five years that there are specific situations that have caused emotional pain to motivate a person not to trust. People who have been abused, whether it be emotionally, physically, sexually or spiritually, are known to have anxiety issues. That makes sense when you think about it for a moment. It feels that there is no one to trust. You may have some trust issues if someone in your family has been an active alcoholic or addict. You may have trust issues if anyone in your environment has been suffering from mental illness. They may or may not know that they are harming you. But you know it and you feel it.

In my situation, it was my father's erratic behavior, his alcoholism, his mental illness and finally attempting to murder my family. Now, I can hear you saying, "Yes that will do it." It certainly will. However, there are plenty of less dramatic scenarios that are emotionally painful when they happen in our lives.

For example, lying to someone can be so painful. We realize that people we know tell lies. But, we don't expect them to tell us a lie. Is that not insanity in our thinking? We have this irrational expectation that although our friend does lie to people, she or he will not lie to us. It hurts when they do. Trust is broken. Your belief in the illusion of their integrity is shattered. Most likely, you forgive them and they do it again and again. At some point, you have to choose not to associate with people who do not live in their integrity! Healthy boundaries are needed to create a safe space in your world so that others do not get the opportunity to break your trust. Learning how to create those healthy boundaries takes time. Why not make it a goal starting today?

Another example is how many of you have loaned a family member or a friend some money? How many of you have had a tough time getting it repaid? Did you notice when they were asking you to loan them money how they worded the request? Think back. Did you notice that quite often, people will say things like, "I will pay you back on such and such date," and then they don't. Or "I am your family" to guilt and manipulate you? Watch how people attempt to manipulate you! They have your trust and they play their cards in the way they know will get you to give them their way.

Trust is built by being honest and being trust worthy. Trust is a confidence or a condition where there is a sacred relationship between the parties. What is between them is the belief that they will keep their word. That has to be nurtured and honored over time to create something substantial. It is incredibly painful otherwise.

When trust is broken our hearts ache. We get wounded and then angry. We want to understand but our fueled by the heat of the moment. Some of us want to retaliate. We want to show them that they can't do this to us! Give that up as soon as you feel it. It is not going to make you feel better.

How do we heal ourselves when we feel that we cannot trust others? The first thing to do is to evaluate who you are spending your time with. Anyone who is in active addiction, in other words, actively using and or abusing their drugs of choice, (yes this includes your very best friend that loves to get high "just on weed") is not to be trusted. I know it is a broad, generalized statement. In this case, attempt to trust me on this issue. Next, create a support system of healthy minded people who are in their integrity and are actively working a spiritual program of some form. The likelihood of you getting hurt is lessened if you learn who it is better for you to be around. Ultimately, you are responsible for how people treat you. There will be plenty waiting to treat you in a hurtful manner if you choose to let folks treat you bad Most importantly, begin the learning process of going within and learning to trust yourself and the God of your understanding. As you begin to grow in this process you will learn amazing bits of knowledge which will help you move forward into your life in a positive direction.

Chapter Seventeen Workbook Exercise

Name three people you can trust.

Name three people in your life you know you cannot trust and why.

Name some folks who you need to apologize to/make amends to and why.

18

HOW TO TRANSFORM YOUR THOUGHTS INTO POWER

Empowerment is seductive. Once you have tasted it you will want more. Being in control of your life is one of the greatest gifts you can give yourself. Moving from a place of fear to a place of strength is incredible. It is a journey of self discovery. You need to know why you feel the way you do so you can make a conscious choice in deciding if it is comes from a place of truth and love or a place of fear.

Each step you take toward your personal freedom makes it a little easier and more comfortable to get to the next step. It is not going to happen overnight. It is a one day at a time journey. Some days it is going to be one moment in the day at a time journey. You will be empowering yourself and building on that foundation each moment you find peace and serenity. A foundation will surely be built by you for you.

How it is built depends on you and your choices. The basis of Transformation is that your own thoughts must change because you want to see things differently.

When you begin the process and the irrational thoughts are flying in your mind you need to breathe deep slowly and gently and tell yourself these thoughts are not true. You have to become aware that you are having them first and foremost. That will be easy to see and feel. Then, you have to discern whether they come from fear or love. The easy test is to ask yourself this question, "Does this thought feel good?" If the answer is "no," then reach for a better feel good thought. A thought is just a thought. You can change it in an instant. Stretch to find thoughts you feel good feeling.

Make a list of positive things about yourself to remind yourself you are a good person. Start with I am the Light. I am loving. I am thoughtful. I am kind. I am compassionate. I share. I am loved. My dog loves me. Make a list. Ask others who love you to help you make a list of good things about you if you find it hard to make a list on your own. Write them down. Keep the list handy for when you feel down or scared or unworthy.

Once you find yourself able to reach for a better thought you are empowering yourself to change. You will have times when you find yourself telling yourself negative stories. Notice when this happens. It happens for me when I am overtired, hungry and lonely. In the 12 Step Recovery community there is a term called HALT. It stands for Hungry, Angry, Lonely, and Tired. We are at our most vulnerable in those situations. When you are beating up on yourself ask yourself if you are Hungry, Angry, Lonely or Tired. Then Halt/stop those messages you are telling yourself and reach for the next better thought about yourself!

Own your personal power and feel your personal empowerment. Give yourself a pat on the back when you are moving through your process. Don't look for perfection. That idea will mess you up all your life. Just be the best you that you can be today. Give yourself love and forgiveness daily. Love unconditionally. Practice kindness. Believe in yourself and in others. Have hope! Dream big dreams. The worst thing in the world might be if your dream came true and you had picked an average dream. The Universe has the unlimited power to help you manifest in your highest and best good. Stay in gratitude. You will sense your power internally. No one will have to stroke your ego if you are intrinsically aware of your power. Go within or you will go without.

I would like to leave you with one of my favorite quotes from Marianne Williamson:

"Our deepest fear is not that we are inadequate. Our deepest fear is that we are powerful beyond measure. It is our light, not our darkness that most frightens us. We ask ourselves, who am I to be brilliant, gorgeous, talented, fabulous? Actually, who are you not to be? You are a child of God. Your playing small does not serve the world. There is nothing enlightened about shrinking so that other people won't feel insecure around you. We are all meant to shine, as children do. We were born to make manifest the glory of God that is within us. It's not just in some of us; it's in everyone. And as we let our own light shine, we unconsciously give other people permission to do the same. As we are liberated from our own fear, our presence automatically liberates others."

I hope this journey on the pathway to healing has provided you with some valuable truths to help you move positively forward on your path. I believe in you!

I send you all my deepest hopes and prayers for you to empower yourself by knowing who you are and finding a spiritual path that helps you feel peace. Be blessed; Blessed be!

WORKBOOK

1. Affirmations

Let's look at your fears. Looking at them takes away some of the power you have given them. I am going to ask you some questions. Fill in your answers either in the book or on your own notebook if you have purchased an ebook. Take a couple of deep breaths when and if resistance comes up. Then go ahead and answer. You will begin to feel the freedom of your own power as you write your answers. Remember, you cannot do this wrong!

Here are the topics for this section:

A. Fear of Success

Example: I am afraid that if I got the job that I really want I might have to move from where I live now.

List your fears of success:

1. _____

2. _____

3. _____

Now, re-read your list. Ask yourself, "Is this true?"

Turn this thought into a positive affirmation about yourself.

Example: I trust that all my needs will be handled easily.

1. _____

2. _____

3. _____

B. Fear of Failure

Fear of failure causes people to choose to not attempt new things. Can you think of situations in your life that you chose not to attempt somthing that you wanted to do?

Example: I didn't apply to go to college because I knew I'd fail.

List some of those now.

1. _____

2. _____

3. _____

This is the beginning of your list. Turn these thoughts around in an affirmation that positively indicates your change in thinking.

1. _____

2. _____

3. _____

C. Fear of not being good enough

We all have struggled with this lie. This fear is powerful in a negative way.

List three things that you have thought that made you think you are not good enough.

Example: I don't make enough money to be happy.

1. _____

2. _____

3. _____

Remember you are a Child of God, The Universe and the Light! You are enough! You are created whole and unconditionally loved!

Turn these fears into a positive affirmation about yourself.

1. _____

2. _____

3. _____

D. Fear of not being loved

This one is a big hurt! We feel the lack of love inside and outside of us. List five reasons you feel that you don't qualify to be loved!

Example: I am too fat to be loved.

1. _____

2. _____

3. _____

Pay attention here! You have so much love to give and recieve that you cannot possibly share it all in your lifetime. Open your heart and let the love in. Accept compliments. Nurture yourself. Don't stay around people who put you down and disrespect you! Ask yourself "Is this really true?"

Now turn these thoughts around!

1. _____

2. _____

3. _____

How are you feeling now? What parts of this exercise gave you a sense of power? Which ones made you feel sad?

Which ones made you feel happy and why?

_____

_____

Take another look at your answers. What have you learned about yourself from this exercise?

_____

_____

_____

Workshop Exercises:

Chapter One Workbook Exercise:

Have you been abused or mistreated? How do you handle the memories that are hurtful? Do you talk to anyone about it? Do you write your thoughts and feelings in a journal? Have you realized that you are not at fault? Do you have some kind of support system to help facilitate healing for you for these situations?

In the notes below answer the questions from above

_____

_____

_____

_____

Chapter Two Workbook Exercises

In the book there are lots of examples of behaviors for people who are emotionally wounded. Review that section and then write down three symptoms or descriptions that you feel define you now. Later you will have the opportunity to go back and review this. You will be able to see and compare the "fear based responses you" to the "you with your positive changes"!

1. _____

2. _____

3. _____

Chapter Three Workbook Exercises

Name some illnesses you have had that you think were brought on by stress, fear or anger. Explain why you think this is true.

Example: I have had anxiety because I do not feel safe out of my comfort zone.

1. _____

2. _____

3. _____

Chapter Four Workbook Exercise

In the book, I encourage you to go to a safe space inside yourself. Take time to to write in your notebook about this experience. How did it feel? Were you afraid you wouldn't be able to get to the safe, calm space? Did you get there? If not, what thoughts were you thinking to stop this from happening? What did it look like? Were things colorful and lush? Was it in black and white? Were other people there?

_____

_____

Chapter Five Workshop Exercise:

Can you name some of the stories that you tell yourself? Name one story about your schooling or work. Name another about your relationships with others. Name a third about your goals and dreams.

1. _____

2. _____

3. _____

Do you want to keep these stories in your life? Do you want to make up a new thought for yourself?

If you want to make up a new story for yourself write the basic narrative here.

1. _____

2. _____

3. _____

Chapter Six Workbook Exercise

You can use the four questions from <u>Loving What Is</u> to get a reality check on your thinking anytime. It is best to practice using it until you know it by heart. Some people like to write the questions down in their cell phone or on a card to put in their pocket. Practice this process with a friend to make it more fun for you. List the four questions in the spaces below to help you remember them.

1. _____

2. _____

3. _____

Chapter Seven Workbook Exercise

Take time out to write down some of your family secrets and unspoken rules. Does that make you feel stressed? Fearful? Anxious? Depressed? What could you do differently NOW that you are in charge of your own thinking? Are there any thoughts you can now discard and be free of? Write down which ones and why.

Family Secrets and Unspoken Rules

_____

_____

_____

Write your thoughts about them now.

_____

_____

_____

What have you learned about your family and yourself in this process?

_____

_____

Chapter Eight Workbook Exercise

Forgiveness heals. Making amends to others makes us fell good in many ways.

Coming from a place of love restores us to sanity.

Name some people you want to forgive and why.

1. _____

2. _____

3. _____

Name some people that you need to ask forgiveness from and why.

1. _____

2. _____

3. _____

Chapter Nine Workbook Exercise

Name three symptoms of depression.

1. _____

2. _____

3. _____

True or False:

1. Depression only happens in adults.

2. Alcohol is not a depressant.

3. Get on anti-depressants and then choose to get off the meds when you feel better.

Chapter Ten Workbook Exercise

Name three ways to decrease stress discussed in this chapter.

1. _____

2. _____

3. _____

True or False

Anxiety attacks are similar to blood sugar attacks. T or F

Name three symptoms of anxiety

_____

_____

_____

What can you tell yourself when you are beginning to have an anxiety or panic attack?

_____

_____

Chapter Eleven Workbook Exercises

Take time to write down your top resentments in your notebook. Take time to look at them and see if you can find a new way to look at them. Write it down to review later.

1. _____

2. _____

3. _____

Take a moment to reflect on the resentments you wrote down earlier. Do you still have any resentments that you have not reconciled in some way. Write them. Share them with someone who supports you emotionally.

1. _____

2. _____

3. _____

Resentments will continue to show up as you grow in your healing process. Just note them, allow them to come to a place of awareness and then get rid of them!

Think about a situation where you blamed someone else. Write down how you could have handled that situation differently.

_____

_____

_____

_____

_____

Guilt eats away at your self confidence and self esteem. Think about when you have chosen to feel guilty over a situation. Name three times where you have placed guilt wrongly. Then explain how you can make it better in the future

1. _____

_____

2. _____

_____

3. _____

_____

Chapter Twelve Workbook Exercises

Make a list of those people you feel you choose to forgive to move forward. Find a quiet place to focus. Say to yourself "I forgive you,_____, for _____. I release you and myself from this negative energy. Go in Peace and Love."

Name three situations or relationships where you need to forgive yourself.

1. _____

2. _____

3. _____

Say to yourself for each situation or relationship "I forgive myself for _____ and release myself from holding this negative energy any longer."

Chapter Thirteen Workbook Exercises

Creating a Gratitude Journal will help you begin finding situations in which to be grateful. Start each day by writing down a few things in your Gratitude Journal See how many different things you can be grateful for in the first week, month and year. You will be amazed at the miracles that begin to show up in your life!

Name three reasons to be grateful today!

1. _____

2. _____

3. _____

Chapter Fourteen Workbook Exercises

Write in your notebook about what a stress free day would look and feel like for you. Remember to add as many details as you can! The aroma of the roses, the smell of a fresh cup of coffee, a warm genuine hug are all details. Take your time and visualize it.

_____

_____

_____

Chapter Fifteen Workbook Exercises

Can you name three things that you would like to manifest into your life by focusing on the positive rather than negative? Do that now.

1. _____

2. _____

3. _____

Chapter Sixteen Workbook Exercises

What is the very first thing we have to do to know we have an addiction problem?

_____

Where can we go if we have an addiction issue?

_____

True or False

Alcoholics can't quit drinking. T or F

12 Step recovery groups are expensive. T or F

Most addicts hate themselves. T or F

Chapter Seventeen Workbook Exercise

Name three people you can trust and why.

1. _____

2. _____

3. _____

Name three people in your life you know you cannot trust and why.

1. _____

2. _____

3. _____

Name some folks you need to apologize to (make amends) and why.

_____

_____

_____

Chapter Eighteen Workbook Exercises

Make a list of positive things about yourself to remind yourself you are a good person. Examples are: I am the Light. I am loving. I am thoughtful. I am kind. I am compassionate. I share. I am loved. My dog loves me. Make a list. Ask others who love you to help you make a list of good things about you if you find it hard to make a list on your own. Write them down. Keep the list handy for when you feel down or scared or unworthy.

1. _____

2. _____

3. _____

4. _____

5. _____

Gratitude Journal

It is easy to create a Gratitude Journal. Get a notebook and inside on the paper write the date of the entry. Then list in your own thoughts specifically what you are grateful for and why. Daily entries can have the same gratitudes listed or different ones. I enjoy seeing how many different things I can be grateful for in a month's time without duplicating them. That is just me. You can create your journal any way you want. It is a blessing to have it to review. It will remind yourself just how good you do have it. Good luck with it!

BIBLIOGRAPHY

A Course in Miracles. Second Revised Edition. Set of 3 Volumes, including, Text, Teacher's Manual, Workbook. Foundation of Inner Peace,*1992*

Anonymous*, Just For Today, Daily Meditations for Recovering Addicts.* Van Nuys, California. Narcotics Anonymous World Services, 1991

Casey, Karen. *Daily Meditations for Practicing the Course.* Center City, Minnesota: Hazelden Publishing, 1995

Fox, Emmet. *The Sermon on the Mount.* San Francisco, California Harper San Francisco, 1989

Hanh, Thich Nhat. *Being Peace.* Berkeley, California: Parallax Press, 1996

Hay, Louise L. *You Can Heal Your Life.* Santa Monica, California: Hay House, 1982

Hicks*,* Esther and Jerry. *The Law of Attraction.* Carlsbad, California: Hay House, 2006

Holmes, Ernest. *Living the Science of Mind.* Marina del Rey, California: 1984

Hooper, Richard. *Jesus, Buddha, Krishna, Lao Tzu The Parallel Sayings.* Sanctuary Publications, 2008

Katie, Byron and Steven Mitchell. *Loving What Is.*New York*:* Three Rivers Press/Random House, 2003

Kushner MG, Sher KJ, Beitman BD. The relation between alcohol problems and the anxiety disorders. *American Journal of Psychiatry*, 1990; 147(6): 685-95.

LeDoux J. Fear and the brain: where have we been, and where are we going? *Biological Psychiatry*, 1998; 44(12): 1229-38.

Lao-Tzu and D.C. Lau *Tao Te Ching.* Baltimore, Maryland, Penguin Books, 1963

Maitreya, The Venerable Balangoda Ananda. *The Dhammapada.* Berkley, California. Parallax Press, 1995

Myss, Caroline. *Anatomy of the Spirit.* New York. Harmony Books/ Random House, 1996

NIMH Webpage. *Anxiety Disorders.* NIMH NeuroSciencs Division Publication, Rockville, Maryland. National Institute of Mental Health, 2012

NIMH Genetics Workgroup. *Genetics and Mental Disorders.* NIH Publication No. 98-4268. Rockville, MD: National Institute of Mental Health, 1998.

Potter - Efron, Ronald and Patricia. *Ending our Resentments.* Minneapolis, Minnesota: Hazelden Recovery, 2003.

Prabhupada, A.C. Bhaktivedanta Swami. *Bhagavad Gita,* New York: Collier Books, 1972

Siegel, Bernie S. Love, Medicine and Miracles. New York: Harper-Collins,1991

The Iversen Associates. *The Four Translation New Testament: Parallel Edition,* New York, 1966

Weiss, Brian L. *Meditation Achieving Inner Peace and Tranquility in Your Life.* Carlsbad, California. Hay House, 2002

West, Georgianna Tree. *Prosperity's Ten Commandments.* Unity Classic Library, *1996*

Williamson, Marianne. *Illuminata A Return to Prayer.* New York, Riverhead Books. 1992

Yogananda, Paramahansa. *In the Sanctuary of the Soul, A Gude to Effective Praying.* Las Angeles, California, Self- Realization Fellowship, Reprinted 1998

Janice Mann is available for private consultations, seminars, workshops and trainings. To get more information on scheduling or to be placed on the email list for book signings and public workshops contact ***JMannconsulting@verizon.net***